11+ Verbal Reasoning
Sequences, Logic & Coding

For **GL** Assessment

These CGP 10-Minute Tests are fully focused on Sequences, Logic and Coding for children aged 9-10 — ideal for building up skills for the GL 11+ test.

We've also included step-by-step answers for every question and a handy chart to track their progress. Nobody does 11+ prep better than CGP!

10-Minute Tests

Ages
9-10

How to access your free Online Edition

This book includes a free Online Edition to read on your PC, Mac or tablet.
You'll just need to go to **cgpbooks.co.uk/extras** and enter this code:

4262 3358 6740 5835

By the way, this code only works for one person. If somebody else has used this book before you, they might have already claimed the Online Edition.

How to use this book

This book is made up of 10-minute tests and puzzle pages.
There are answers and detailed explanations at the back of the book.

10-Minute Tests

- There are 31 tests in this book, each containing either 14 or 16 questions.
  These tests provide bite-sized practice for specific skills tested in the full-length 11+ test.

- Each test is targeted to cover a range of sequence, logic and coding question styles that
  your child could come across in their 11+ test, at just the right level for ages 9-10.

- Your child should aim to score at least 12 out of 14 or 14 out of 16 in each 10-minute test.
  If they score less than this, use their results to work out the areas they need more practice on.

- If your child hasn't managed to finish the test in time, they need to work on increasing their
  speed, whereas if they have made a lot of mistakes, they need to work more carefully.

- Keep track of your child's scores using the progress chart at the back of the book.

Puzzle Pages

- There are 8 puzzle pages in this book, which are a great break from test-style questions.
  They encourage children to practise the same skills that they will need in the test,
  but in a fun way.

Published by CGP

Editors:
Andy Cashmore, Emma Cleasby, Andy Park, Katya Parkes, Sean Walsh, Adam Worster

With thanks to Holly Robinson for the proofreading.

Please note that CGP is not associated with GL Assessment in any way.
This book does not include any official questions and is not endorsed by GL Assessment.

ISBN: 978 1 78908 502 0
Printed by Sterling, Kettering.
Clipart from Corel®

Based on the classic CGP style created by Richard Parsons.

Contents

Test 1 2

Test 2 5

Test 3 7

Puzzles 1 .... **9**

Test 4 10

Test 5 13

Test 6 15

Test 7 17

Puzzles 2 .... **19**

Test 8 20

Test 9 22

Test 10 25

Test 11 28

Puzzles 3 .... **30**

Test 12 31

Test 13 33

Test 14 36

Test 15 38

Puzzles 4 .... **40**

Test 16 41

Test 17 43

Test 18 45

Test 19 48

Puzzles 5 .... **50**

Test 20 51

Test 21 54

Test 22 57

Test 23 59

Puzzles 6 .... **61**

Test 24 62

Test 25 64

Test 26 67

Test 27 69

Puzzles 7 .... **72**

Test 28 73

Test 29 75

Test 30 77

Test 31 79

Puzzles 8 .... **82**

Answers **83**

Progress Chart **100**

You have **10 minutes** to do this test. Work as quickly and accurately as you can.

Find the number that continues each sequence in the best way. Write your answer on the line.

Example: 3   6   9   12   15   (__18__)

1.   7   15   23   31   39   (________)

2.   13   18   22   25   27   (________)

3.   49   11   51   22   53   44   (________)

4.   15   21   18   24   21   (________)

Each question uses a different code. Use the alphabet to help you work out the answer to each question.

A B C D E F G H I J K L M N O P Q R S T U V W X Y Z

Example: If the code for **MANY** is **LZMX**, what is the code for **GREY**? (__FQDX__)

5.   If the code for **DWARF** is **FYCTH**, what is **RCKPV** the code for? (____________)

6.   If the code for **MEAL** is **PADH**, what is **PQFD** the code for? (____________)

7.   If the code for **FARM** is **KEWQ**, what is the code for **HAIL**? (____________)

8.   If the code for **GONE** is **HQQI**, what is the code for **LAMB**? (____________)

Each letter stands for a number. Work out the answer to each sum as a letter.
Write your answer on the line.

Example: A = 1 B = 2 C = 6 D = 12 E = 10   D ÷ B = (_C_)

9.   A = 2   B = 8   C = 9   D = 15   E = 18   E ÷ C = (_______)

10. A = 2   B = 5   C = 9   D = 10   E = 14   C + D − E = (_______)

11. A = 2   B = 5   C = 6   D = 7   E = 28   E ÷ D + A = (_______)

12. A = 4   B = 5   C = 6   D = 25   E = 26   D ÷ B × A + C = (_______)

Read the information carefully, then use it to answer the question that follows.

13. Saiesha, Nabeel, Adam, Tyron and Julian had a contest to see who could throw
     a tennis ball the highest. Adam threw the ball higher than Saiesha. Julian
     threw the ball 20 metres high, which was not as high as Tyron's throw. Saiesha
     threw the ball higher than Tyron. Nabeel had the highest throw.

     If the statements above are true, only one of the sentences below **must** be true.
     Which one? Circle the correct letter.

     A   No one threw the ball higher than Adam.
     B   Tyron had the second highest throw.
     C   Saiesha had the third highest throw.
     D   Nabeel's throw was lower than Julian's.
     E   Saiesha had the lowest throw.

14. Charli, Dean, Yekta, Matt and Alisa are comparing how much homework they have. Dean and Yekta have history homework. Alisa and Matt have geography and English homework. Charli and Matt have science homework. Dean and Matt are the only two who do not have maths homework. No one gets any other homework.

If the statements above are true, only one of the sentences below **must** be true. Which one? Circle the correct letter.

A   Matt and Alisa have homework for the exact same subjects.

B   One more person has history homework than science homework.

C   Dean has homework for two fewer subjects than Alisa.

D   Charli receives three pieces of homework.

E   Yekta and Dean have the same amount of homework.

END OF TEST

/ 14

Test 2

You have **10 minutes** to do this test. Work as quickly and accurately as you can.

Find the number that continues each sequence in the best way. Write your answer on the line.

Example: 3   6   9   12   15   (__18__)

---

1.   50   46   42   38   34   (_______)

2.   62   61   59   56   52   (_______)

3.   96   48   24   12   6   (_______)

4.   18   8   15   10   12   12   (_______)

5.   18   15   19   16   20   (_______)

The number codes for three of these four words are listed in a random order. Work out the code to answer the questions. Write your answer on the line.

HELP   **SELL**   **LASH**   **HEAL**
5261   **6355**   **1354**

6.   Find the code for the word **HEAL**.   (__________)

7.   Find the code for the word **PALE**.   (__________)

8.   Find the word that has the number code **5246**.   (__________)

Each letter stands for a number. Work out the answer to each sum as a letter. Write your answer on the line.

Example: A = 1   B = 2   C = 6   D = 12   E = 10   D ÷ B = (__C__)

9.   A = 5   B = 8   C = 10   D = 13   E = 14   D – A = (________)

10.   A = 4   B = 5   C = 9   D = 13   E = 16   E ÷ A + B = (________)

11.   A = 2   B = 6   C = 9   D = 10   E = 11   D × A – E = (________)

12.   A = 4   B = 6   C = 7   D = 11   E = 20   E ÷ A + C – B = (________)

Each question uses a different code. Use the alphabet to help you work out the answer to each question.

A B C D E F G H I J K L M N O P Q R S T U V W X Y Z

Example: If the code for **MANY** is **LZMX**, what is the code for **GREY**? (FQDX)

13.   If the code for **DOING** is **HSMRK**, what is the code for **COAST**? (___________)

14.   If the code for **GRUMP** is **LNZIU**, what is **MKNOY** the code for? (___________)

15.   If the code for **MORPH** is **RQWRM**, what is the code for **FLASK**? (___________)

16.   If the code for **ROAM** is **QOBO**, what is the code for **CREW**? (___________)

END OF TEST

/ 16

You have **10 minutes** to do this test. Work as quickly and accurately as you can.

Find the missing number to complete each sum. Write your answer on the line.

Example: $7 + 5 = 24 \div ($ __2__ $)$

---

1. $8 \times 6 = ($ _______ $)$

2. $9 \div 3 + 8 = ($ _______ $)$

3. $7 \times 2 = 21 - ($ _______ $)$

4. $19 - 14 = 25 \div ($ _______ $)$

Underline the pair of letters that completes each sentence in the most sensible way. Use the alphabet to help you.

A B C D E F G H I J K L M N O P Q R S T U V W X Y Z

Example: **DG** is to **FE** as **RU** is to (<u>TS</u>   SR   TU   ST   US).

---

5.   **BG** is to **CK** as **ST** is to (TU   TY   TX   UV   UX).

6.   **LM** is to **HH** as **OT** is to (KP   KO   JR   KQ   JN).

7.   **VF** is to **SK** as **HC** is to (EI   BH   BK   CH   EH).

8.   **TM** is to **GN** as **EC** is to (VX   XX   YY   WY   VZ).

Find the pair of letters that continues each sequence in the best way. Use the alphabet to help you.

A B C D E F G H I J K L M N O P Q R S T U V W X Y Z

Example: TU   QR   NO   KL   HI   (__EF__)

9.   JM   EH   ZC   UX   PS   (______)

10. LG   MJ   NM   OP   PS   (______)

11. FC   KH   NK   SP   VS   (______)

12. ES   HW   CB   FF   AK   (______)

Find the number that completes the final set of numbers in the same way as the first two sets. Write your answer on the line.

Example: 7 (4) 3   10 (5) 5   15 (__11__) 4

13. 12 (2) 6   50 (10) 5   16 (______) 4

14. 3 (9) 3   4 (8) 2   7 (______) 4

15. 4 (14) 5   2 (10) 4   2 (______) 2

16. 9 (10) 4   8 (14) 1   10 (______) 6

END OF TEST

/ 16

Let's give these puzzles a whirl! They'll test your **sequencing** and **maths** skills.

Confusing Kassaqr

A group of cousins have invented a new language called Kassaqr so
they can write secret notes to each other about the sports they play.
Work out the sequence so that you can read the first line of the secret note.

A B C D E F G H I J K L M N O P Q R S T U V W X Y Z

Diiszukk is the word for football.
Gibjax is the word for hockey.
Rpourg is the word for squash.

Think about how the patterns for vowels and consonants are different.

Cauq Allu, E vim sga fula!

_____ _____, __ ____

____ _____!

Wriggling Wes

Wes the Worm has eaten through 12 books to reach a juicy apple.

It took Wes **two minutes** to eat through each Book A, which was
shorter than the **three minutes** it took to eat through each Book B.
Each Book C took Wes **four minutes** to eat through, but he also
needed a **five minute** break after every Book C.

How long did it take Wes to reach the apple?

It took Wes ________ minutes.

You have **10 minutes** to do this test. Work as quickly and accurately as you can.

> Find the number that completes the final set of numbers in the same way as the first two sets. Write your answer on the line.
>
> **Example:**   7 (4) 3   10 (5) 5   15 (__11__) 4

1.   20 (5) 4   18 (9) 2   24 (_______) 4

2.   7 (11) 4   5 (9) 4   2 (_______) 7

3.   6 (4) 2   11 (9) 2   17 (_______) 8

4.   9 (12) 1   10 (21) 9   8 (_______) 1

> Read the information carefully, then use it to answer the question that follows.

5.   Edward, Nikita, Brendan, Camilla and Luke want to see who has the tallest cat. Luke's cat is 15 cm tall and half the height of Edward's cat. Camilla's cat is taller than Edward's. Brendan's cat is shorter than Luke's. Nikita's cat is 5 cm shorter than Edward's.

If the statements above are true, only one of the sentences below **must** be true. Which one? Circle the correct letter.

   A   Camilla has the second tallest cat.

   B   Nikita's cat is 20 cm tall.

   C   Camilla's cat is shorter than Nikita's.

   D   Brendan's cat is shorter than Edward's.

   E   Luke and Camilla's cats are related.

6. Clara, Sharif, Freya, Lucas and Bradley are comparing which albums they
own. Freya is the only one who doesn't own 'I'm Here'. Bradley and Lucas
own 'Look Back' and 'The Zebra Album'. Freya also owns 'The Zebra Album'.
Clara and Sharif own 'Plant Life', but Clara also owns 'Hit It'. No one owns
any other albums.

If the statements above are true, only one of the sentences below **cannot** be true.
Which one? Circle the correct letter.

A Lucas owns two albums that Sharif does not own.

B Only one person owns 'Hit It'.

C Clara's favourite album is 'Plant Life'.

D Sharif owns the fewest albums.

E 'The Zebra Album' is owned by one more person than 'Look Back'.

Find the pair of letters that continues each sequence in the best way. Use the
alphabet to help you.

A B C D E F G H I J K L M N O P Q R S T U V W X Y Z

Example: TU   QR   NO   KL   HI   (___EF___)

---

7. IM   NR   SW   XB   CG   (______)

8. QP   RM   SJ   TG   UD   (______)

9. LH   HD   KG   GC   JF   (______)

10. JY   LV   HT   JQ   FO   (______)

11.   **JC** is to **LF** as **PI** is to   (RK   RO   RL   UL   SO).

12.   **PU** is to **OQ** as **IZ** is to   (HW   HV   IU   GV   FY).

13.   **VU** is to **TY** as **NX** is to   (JC   IB   LZ   LB   LA).

14.   **KW** is to **PD** as **CM** is to   (WP   VN   ZM   XN   XP).

END OF TEST

/ 14

You have **10 minutes** to do this test. Work as quickly and accurately as you can.

Find the number that continues each sequence in the best way. Write your answer on the line.

Example: 3   6   9   12   15   (__18__)

1.   43   35   27   19   11   (_______)

2.   54   9   50   7   46   5   (_______)

3.   50   40   32   26   22   (_______)

4.   5   8   18   21   31   (_______)

Underline the pair of letters that completes each sentence in the most sensible way. Use the alphabet to help you.

A B C D E F G H I J K L M N O P Q R S T U V W X Y Z

Example: **DG** is to **FE** as **RU** is to (<u>TS</u>   SR   TU   ST   US).

5.   **EJ** is to **GO** as **VF** is to   (WL   WK   UN   XJ   XK).

6.   **IR** is to **EP** as **YC** is to   (UE   WZ   VA   UA   UC).

7.   **KR** is to **MO** as **JH** is to   (LE   ME   OB   LH   OE).

8.   **OX** is to **LC** as **AI** is to   (ZR   BQ   YS   XR   ZT).

Find the missing number to complete each sum. Write your answer on the line.

Example: $7 + 5 = 24 \div ($ ___2___ $)$

9. $37 + 5 = ($ _______ $)$

10. $4 \times 7 - 5 = ($ _______ $)$

11. $13 + 14 - 8 = ($ _______ $)$

12. $10 + 21 = 39 - ($ _______ $)$

Each question uses a different code. Use the alphabet to help you work out the answer to each question.

A B C D E F G H I J K L M N O P Q R S T U V W X Y Z

Example: If the code for **MANY** is **LZMX**, what is the code for **GREY**? (__FQDX__)

13.   If the code for **SHADE** is **UJCFG**, what is **LQMGT** the code for? (___________)

14.   If the code for **POLE** is **NTJJ**, what is **ATKG** the code for? (___________)

15.   If the code for **SOUL** is **VTXQ**, what is the code for **PARK**? (___________)

16.   If the code for **ALIGN** is **CMIFL**, what is the code for **QUEST**? (___________)

END OF TEST

/ 16

You have **10 minutes** to do this test. Work as quickly and accurately as you can.

The number codes for three of these four words are listed in a random order.
Work out the code to answer the questions. Write your answer on the line.

CENT   THEN   CITE   CHIN
6415   6342   1352

1.   Find the code for the word **CENT**.   (___________)

2.   Find the code for the word **TENT**.   (___________)

3.   Find the word that has the number code **3421**. (___________)

Each letter stands for a number. Work out the answer to each sum as a letter.
Write your answer on the line.

Example: $A = 1$ $B = 2$ $C = 6$ $D = 12$ $E = 10$ $D \div B = ($ __C__ $)$

4. $A = 3$ $B = 4$ $C = 9$ $D = 12$ $E = 27$ $D \div A = ($ _______ $)$

5. $A = 3$ $B = 9$ $C = 10$ $D = 12$ $E = 18$ $C \times A - D = ($ _______ $)$

6. $A = 3$ $B = 6$ $C = 8$ $D = 12$ $E = 14$ $D + C - B = ($ _______ $)$

7. $A = 3$ $B = 8$ $C = 10$ $D = 16$ $E = 24$ $E \div A + B = ($ _______ $)$

8. $A = 5$ $B = 10$ $C = 11$ $D = 31$ $E = 40$ $E \div B \times A + C = ($ _______ $)$

Each question uses a different code. Use the alphabet to help you work out the answer to each question.

A B C D E F G H I J K L M N O P Q R S T U V W X Y Z

Example: If the code for **MANY** is **LZMX**, what is the code for **GREY**? (<u>FQDX</u>)

9.   If the code for **FLOUR** is **BHKQN**, what is the code for **YOUNG**?   (____________)

10.   If the code for **GECKO** is **HCDIP**, what is **BUGSM** the code for?   (____________)

11.   If the code for **DANCE** is **HCREI**, what is the code for **SOLID**?   (____________)

12.   If the code for **RUNT** is **PRJO**, what is **RLHG** the code for?   (____________)

Find the pair of letters that continues each sequence in the best way. Use the alphabet to help you.

A B C D E F G H I J K L M N O P Q R S T U V W X Y Z

Example: TU   QR   NO   KL   HI   (<u>EF</u>)

13.   DI   GL   JO   MR   PU   (______)

14.   SH   PK   MN   JQ   GT   (______)

15.   HA   IB   LE   MF   PI   (______)

16.   QR   NO   SL   PI   UF   (______)

END OF TEST

/ 16

Test 7

You have **10 minutes** to do this test. Work as quickly and accurately as you can.

Find the number that continues each sequence in the best way. Write your answer on the line.

Example: 3   6   9   12   15   (__18__)

1.   4   13   22   31   40   (_______)

2.   47   40   37   39   27   38   (_______)

3.   41   46   50   53   55   (_______)

4.   73   71   70   70   71   (_______)

5.   11   14   22   25   33   (_______)

The number codes for three of these four words are listed in a random order. Work out the code to answer the questions. Write your answer on the line.

SAIL   SLIT   SITS   HILT
5431   6312   5325

6.   Find the code for the word **SAIL**.   (__________)

7.   Find the code for the word **HALT**.   (__________)

8.   Find the word that has the number code **1452**. (__________)

                17

Underline the pair of letters that completes each sentence in the most sensible way. Use the alphabet to help you.

A B C D E F G H I J K L M N O P Q R S T U V W X Y Z

Example: **DG** is to **FE** as **RU** is to (<u>TS</u> SR TU ST US).

9. **TU** is to **WZ** as **AC** is to (EE   EI   EH   DE   DH).

10. **ON** is to **MI** as **HP** is to (FK   FJ   IJ   GK   FL).

11. **DJ** is to **FE** as **QP** is to   (VK   UN   SL   UK   SK).

12. **NF** is to **MU** as **DB** is to (WW WY   XW   UW   UY).

Each letter stands for a number. Work out the answer to each sum as a letter. Write your answer on the line.

Example: A = 1 B = 2 C = 6 D = 12 E = 10   D ÷ B = (_____C_____)

13. A = 1   B = 6   C = 13   D = 14   E = 19   E − B = (_________)

14. A = 4   B = 7   C = 8   D = 9   E = 27   E ÷ D + A = (_________)

15. A = 3   B = 4   C = 7   D = 9   E = 13   D + C − E = (_________)

16. A = 3   B = 5   C = 6   D = 10   E = 24   E ÷ C + B − A = (_________)

END OF TEST

/ 16

It's puzzle time! Have a go at these to test your **coding** and **riddle-solving** skills.

Pirate Pop Songs

Percy the Pirate remembers the lyrics to his favourite songs by changing the words into number codes. Use the clue words in the box to work out the pattern in the numbers. Then, work out what Percy is singing about.

26897	27732	41753
SEEDS	BREAD	SUITE

461873   91752617

___ ___ ___ ___ ___ ___   ___ ___ ___ ___ ___ ___ ___ ___

A Case for Cluelo

Detective Cluelo is trying to find out who painted over a picture in the art gallery. She has statements from five suspects, but she knows the guilty person is lying.

Nisha — *"I was looking at a map because Pablo had got us lost in the gallery."*

Claude — *"Melina and I left to get some food after we were told everything above Floor 4 was closed."*

Pablo — *"Nisha and I were moving between exhibits, but I did spot Melina going down the stairs in a hurry."*

Georgia — *"After seeing the sculptures, I went to the rooftop cafe for a drink."*

Melina — *"I left the gallery with Claude to get lunch — I was starving!"*

Who do you think painted over the picture? ___________________

You have **10 minutes** to do this test. Work as quickly and accurately as you can.

Underline the pair of letters that completes each sentence in the most sensible way. Use the alphabet to help you.

A B C D E F G H I J K L M N O P Q R S T U V W X Y Z

Example: DG is to **FE** as **RU** is to (TS SR TU ST US).

1. **TR** is to **YW** as **FE** is to (KJ   LJ   KM   KI   NH).

2. **BR** is to **EV** as **OM** is to (QS   TR   RQ   RR   QQ).

3. **KF** is to **JC** as **OX** is to (NU   MV   MU   OV   NV).

4. **YC** is to **UH** as **EH** is to (BN   AL   ZJ   AM   AO).

Find the number that continues each sequence in the best way. Write your answer on the line.

Example: 3   6   9   12   15   (___18___)

5.   41   34   27   20   13   (________)

6.   98   97   95   92   88   (________)

7.   19   17   22   13   25   9   (________)

8.   6   9   14   17   22   (________)

Find the missing number to complete each sum. Write your answer on the line.

Example: $7 + 5 = 24 \div ($ __2__ $)$

9. $29 + 12 = ($ _______ $)$

10. $88 \div 8 + 9 = ($ _______ $)$

11. $14 + 17 - 3 = ($ _______ $)$

12. $18 \div 3 = 2 \times ($ _______ $)$

Each question uses a different code. Use the alphabet to help you work out the answer to each question.

A B C D E F G H I J K L M N O P Q R S T U V W X Y Z

Example: If the code for **MANY** is **LZMX**, what is the code for **GREY**? (__FQDX__)

13. If the code for **RATED** is **UDWHG**, what is the code for **BRICK**? (___________)

14. If the code for **SHUN** is **QKSQ**, what is **BDPN** the code for? (___________)

15. If the code for **DIET** is **AHBS**, what is the code for **WORM**? (___________)

16. If the code for **MOAT** is **NQDX**, what is the code for **PURE**? (___________)

END OF TEST

/ 16

You have **10 minutes** to do this test. Work as quickly and accurately as you can.

Find the pair of letters that continues each sequence in the best way. Use the alphabet to help you.

A B C D E F G H I J K L M N O P Q R S T U V W X Y Z

Example: TU   QR   NO   KL   HI   (__EF__)

---

1.   VN   SK   PH   ME   JB   (______)

2.   SX   RT   QP   PL   OH   (______)

3.   KH   JK   IN   HQ   GT   (______)

4.   FC   HE   KH   MJ   PM   (______)

5.   TC   RE   PF   NF   LE   (______)

Each letter stands for a number. Work out the answer to each sum as a letter. Write your answer on the line.

Example: A = 1   B = 2   C = 6   D = 12   E = 10 $D \div B = ($ __C__ $)$

---

6.   A = 3   B = 11   C = 12   D = 14   E = 36 $E \div A = ($ ________ $)$

7.   A = 6   B = 7   C = 9   D = 12   E = 15 $C + D - A = ($ ________ $)$

8.   A = 5   B = 9   C = 10   D = 12   E = 14 $C + B - E = ($ ________ $)$

9.   A = 4   B = 7   C = 9   D = 15   E = 18 $E \div C \times A + B = ($ ________ $)$

10. Jeandre, Tay, Devveena, Lorne and Erik want to find out who can read the most books over the summer. Tay reads nine books. Erik reads three more books than Tay. Devveena reads one book fewer than Tay. Lorne reads two more books than Devveena. Jeandre reads fewer books than Erik, but more than Lorne.

If the statements above are true, only one of the sentences below **cannot** be true. Which one? Circle the correct letter.

A   Jeandre reads 11 books.

B   Lorne reads fewer books than Erik.

C   Lorne enjoys reading more than Jeandre.

D   Erik reads fewer books than Devveena.

E   Erik reads 12 books.

11. Tasha, Justin, Faisal, Ellie and Megan all own stickers from a book. There are five different stickers. Ellie and Justin own sticker one. Faisal owns stickers three and four. Megan owns sticker four, and both her and Justin own sticker five. Tasha owns a sticker that none of the others have. No one owns any other stickers.

If the statements above are true, only one of the sentences below **cannot** be true. Which one? Circle the correct letter.

A   Tasha owns sticker two.

B   Three people own more stickers than Ellie.

C   Faisal's favourite sticker is sticker four.

D   Megan and Justin own the same number of stickers.

E   Only one sticker is owned by just one person.

BEST   BASE   OATS   TOES
3524   4152   3625

12. Find the code for the word **OATS**.   (___________)

13. Find the code for the word **OBOE**.   (___________)

14. Find the word that has the number code **4632**. (___________)

END OF TEST

/ 14

You have **10 minutes** to do this test. Work as quickly and accurately as you can.

Find the number that completes the final set of numbers in the same way as the first two sets. Write your answer on the line.

Example: 7 (4) 3   10 (5) 5   15 (__11__) 4

---

1.   5 (3) 2   10 (5) 5   9 (_______) 2

2.   10 (18) 8   6 (9) 3   4 (_______) 9

3.   5 (7) 3   10 (18) 2   3 (_______) 1

4.   4 (19) 5   10 (59) 6   5 (_______) 3

Find the pair of letters that continues each sequence in the best way. Use the alphabet to help you.

A B C D E F G H I J K L M N O P Q R S T U V W X Y Z

Example: TU   QR   NO   KL   HI   (__EF__)

---

5.   ZU   VQ   RM   NI   JE   (_______)

6.   NR   PO   RL   TI   VF   (_______)

7.   TG   QD   SF   PC   RE   (_______)

8.   QC   PE   NG   KI   GK   (_______)

Each letter stands for a number. Work out the answer to each sum as a letter.
Write your answer on the line.

Example: A = 1   B = 2   C = 6   D = 12   E = 10   D ÷ B = (__C__)

9.   A = 5   B = 6   C = 12   D = 13   E = 18   E – C = (________)

10.   A = 2   B = 5   C = 8   D = 11   E = 13   C + B – D = (________)

11.   A = 2   B = 4   C = 8   D = 11   E = 16   C × B – E = (________)

12.   A = 3   B = 4   C = 5   D = 7   E = 15   E ÷ A + C – D = (________)

Read the information carefully, then use it to answer the question that follows.

13.   Lace, Rose, Nick, Dale and Amica are competing to swim the most laps of a
      swimming pool. Amica swam 40 laps, which was double the amount of laps
      that Lace swam. Lace swam three more laps than Nick. Rose swam fewer laps
      than Nick. Dale swam five laps more than Lace.

      If the statements above are true, only one of the sentences below **must** be true.
      Which one? Circle the correct letter.

      A   Dale swam 25 laps.

      B   Rose swam more than 20 laps.

      C   Amica swam fewer laps than Lace.

      D   Dale swam 10 laps more than Amica.

      E   Nick swam the most laps.

14. Rob, Ling, Bill, Isla and Simon get dressed to go to the beach. Bill wears a swimming costume and goggles. Simon only wears a hat and shorts. Ling wears four items of clothing, which is the most worn by anyone. Isla wears one fewer item of clothing than Ling. Rob is the only person to wear trunks and only wears two items of clothing. Isla doesn't wear shorts. No one wears any other items of clothing.

If the statements above are true, only one of the sentences below **must** be true. Which one? Circle the correct letter.

A   Ling and Simon wear the same types of clothing.

B   Rob wears more clothing than Simon.

C   All five of them wear goggles.

D   Isla wears a swimming costume, goggles and a hat.

E   Ling owns the most colourful hat.

END OF TEST

/ 14

You have **10 minutes** to do this test. Work as quickly and accurately as you can.

Each letter stands for a number. Work out the answer to each sum as a letter.
Write your answer on the line.

Example: $A = 1$ $B = 2$ $C = 6$ $D = 12$ $E = 10$ $D \div B = ($ ___C___ $)$

---

1. $A = 3$ $B = 7$ $C = 13$ $D = 15$ $E = 28$ $C + D = ($ ________ $)$

2. $A = 5$ $B = 9$ $C = 10$ $D = 14$ $E = 25$ $E \div A + B = ($ ________ $)$

3. $A = 2$ $B = 5$ $C = 9$ $D = 12$ $E = 14$ $A + D - B = ($ ________ $)$

4. $A = 5$ $B = 6$ $C = 9$ $D = 12$ $E = 13$ $D + B - E = ($ ________ $)$

5. $A = 2$ $B = 5$ $C = 9$ $D = 15$ $E = 18$ $E \div C \times A + B = ($ ________ $)$

Find the missing number to complete each sum. Write your answer on the line.

Example: $7 + 5 = 24 \div ($ ___2___ $)$

---

6. $81 \div 9 = ($ _______ $)$

7. $36 \div 6 - 2 = ($ _______ $)$

8. $20 + 11 - 15 = ($ _______ $)$

9. $7 + 17 = 8 \times ($ _______ $)$

LOAF   **FALL**   **OATH**   **HALF**
5364   **1532**   **2311**

10.   Find the code for the word **HALF**.   (___________)

11.   Find the code for the word **FOOT**.   (___________)

12.   Find the word that has the number code **2136**. (___________)

13.   37   33   29   25   21   (_______)

14.   3   7   14   18   25   (_______)

15.   22   27   31   34   36   (_______)

16.   50   3   44   8   38   13   (_______)

END OF TEST

/ 16

You've definitely earned a break! Give your **number** and **sequencing** skills a test.

Candy Conundrum

A sweetshop has a game where you work out the number of sweets in a jar.
The number of sweets in each large jar can be worked out by using the number
of sweets in the small jars either side of it. Jars on the same shelf use the same
pattern, but each shelf has a different pattern. Complete the unlabelled jars.

Bhavesh's Bikes

Bhavesh packs bike parts. He times how long it takes to pack
different bike parts. Look at the patterns below to find out
how many of each part Bhavesh will pack in 60 minutes.

Bike Part	10 minutes	20 minutes	30 minutes	40 minutes	50 minutes	60 minutes
Wheel	50	100	150	200	250	
Chain	75	150	225	300	375	
Helmet	31	62	93	124	155	
Saddle	45	85	120	150	175	
Bell	100	202	306	412	520	

You have **10 minutes** to do this test. Work as quickly and accurately as you can.

Find the number that completes the final set of numbers in the same way as the first two sets. Write your answer on the line.

Example: 7 (4) 3   10 (5) 5   15 (__11__) 4

---

1.   12 (3) 4   16 (2) 8   77 (_______) 11

2.   4 (6) 2   6 (11) 5   9 (_______) 10

3.   5 (40) 8   7 (28) 4   3 (_______) 9

4.   9 (6) 2   8 (4) 3   10 (_______) 7

Each question uses a different code. Use the alphabet to help you work out the answer to each question.

A B C D E F G H I J K L M N O P Q R S T U V W X Y Z

Example: If the code for **MANY** is **LZMX**, what is the code for **GREY**? (__FQDX__)

---

5.   If the code for **ROVES** is **PMTCQ**, what is **QJGAI** the code for? (___________)

6.   If the code for **POWER** is **RTYJT**, what is **OFINE** the code for? (___________)

7.   If the code for **MISTY** is **LLRWX**, what is the code for **VALUE**? (___________)

8.   If the code for **SILKY** is **HROPB**, what is **JFRGV** the code for? (___________)

Each letter stands for a number. Work out the answer to each sum as a letter.
Write your answer on the line.

Example: A = 1   B = 2   C = 6   D = 12   E = 10   D ÷ B = (___C___)

9.   A = 5   B = 11   C = 14   D = 16   E = 18   A + B = (________)

10.   A = 3   B = 5   C = 7   D = 10   E = 28   E ÷ C + A = (________)

11.   A = 4   B = 5   C = 8   D = 13   E = 20   E ÷ B + A = (________)

12.   A = 2   B = 6   C = 8   D = 10   E = 16   A × B + D − E = (________)

Find the number that continues each sequence in the best way. Write your
answer on the line.

Example: 3   6   9   12   15   (___18___)

13.   33   27   21   15   9   (________)

14.   28   29   31   34   38   (________)

15.   29   54   23   44   17   34   (________)

16.   12   20   15   23   18   (________)

END OF TEST

/ 16

(10)

You have **10 minutes** to do this test. Work as quickly and accurately as you can.

Find the pair of letters that continues each sequence in the best way. Use the alphabet to help you.

A B C D E F G H I J K L M N O P Q R S T U V W X Y Z

Example: TU   QR   NO   KL   HI   (__EF__)

---

1.   IJ   LM   OP   RS   UV   (______)

2.   ED   GG   IJ   KM   MP   (______)

3.   ZW   YS   XO   WK   VG   (______)

4.   MY   LX   HT   GS   CO   (______)

5.   LP   KK   JG   ID   HB   (______)

Find the missing number to complete each sum. Write your answer on the line.

Example: $7 + 5 = 24 \div (\underline{\ 2\ })$

---

6. $36 \div 12 = (\underline{\hspace{1cm}})$

7. $18 \div 2 + 3 = (\underline{\hspace{1cm}})$

8. $8 \times 4 = 37 - (\underline{\hspace{1cm}})$

9. $9 \times 2 - 5 = 4 + (\underline{\hspace{1cm}})$

YEAR   MARE   YARD   ARMY
2563   6312   2634

10. Find the code for the word **ARMY**.   (__________)

11. Find the code for the word **RARE**.   (__________)

12. Find the word that has the number code **3564**. (__________)

13. Beth, Li, Susan, Jason and Emma wanted to see who could hold their breath for the longest time. Li held his breath for 65 seconds. Beth held her breath for five seconds less than Li but for twice as long as Jason. Emma did not hold her breath for the shortest time. Susan managed to hold her breath for 25 seconds.

If the statements above are true, only one of the sentences below **must** be true. Which one? Circle the correct letter.

A   Beth held her breath for 45 seconds.

B   Susan held her breath for the shortest time.

C   Li held his breath for a shorter time than Jason.

D   Emma held her breath for a shorter time than Jason.

E   Jason held his breath for 35 seconds.

14. Vicky, Josh, Buhle, Steven and Jess are talking about their favourite foods.
Everyone except Vicky and Josh likes hamburgers. Steven and Buhle like curry,
but they are the only ones who don't like pizza. Josh is the only person who
likes falafel. Vicky likes lasagne and curry. No other foods were mentioned.

If the statements above are true, only one of the sentences below **must** be true.
Which one? Circle the correct letter.

A   One other type of food is more popular than curry.

B   Josh likes more types of food than Buhle.

C   Vicky only likes three of the foods that are talked about.

D   Lasagne is the only food that is liked by just one person.

E   Jess likes hamburgers but not pizza.

END OF TEST

/ 14

You have **10 minutes** to do this test. Work as quickly and accurately as you can.

Underline the pair of letters that completes each sentence in the most sensible way. Use the alphabet to help you.

A B C D E F G H I J K L M N O P Q R S T U V W X Y Z

Example: **DG** is to **FE** as **RU** is to (<u>TS</u> SR TU ST US).

---

1. **NO** is to **RS** as **BM** is to (CQ FQ FR GQ FP).

2. **PD** is to **TI** as **CU** is to (GZ GW IZ GA IW).

3. **IS** is to **ER** as **TK** is to (SL SJ QI PG PJ).

4. **GB** is to **EE** as **MC** is to (KH MG KF LD KG).

Find the number that continues each sequence in the best way. Write your answer on the line.

Example: 3   6   9   12   15   (___18___)

---

5.   1   2   4   8   16   (_______)

6.   46   48   51   55   60   (_______)

7.   44   5   46   10   48   20   (_______)

8.   5   14   10   19   15   (_______)

9. $37 - 12 = ($ _______ $)$

10. $80 \div 10 + 15 = ($ _______ $)$

11. $28 \div 4 = 5 + ($ _______ $)$

12. $22 + 3 - 10 = 5 \times ($ _______ $)$

13.   If the code for **THUMB** is **VJWOD**, what is the code for **CRAWL**? (___________)

14.   If the code for **LANE** is **OEQI**, what is **VPXK** the code for? (___________)

15.   If the code for **LEAP** is **MHBS**, what is the code for **MORE**? (___________)

16.   If the code for **CLIP** is **XORK**, what is **OLHV** the code for? (___________)

END OF TEST

/ 16

You have **10 minutes** to do this test. Work as quickly and accurately as you can.

Each letter stands for a number. Work out the answer to each sum as a letter.
Write your answer on the line.

Example: A = 1 B = 2 C = 6 D = 12 E = 10   D ÷ B = (___C___)

---

1.   A = 5   B = 6   C = 10   D = 13   E = 19   E – D = (_________)

2.   A = 2   B = 3   C = 6   D = 11   E = 30   E ÷ C – B = (________)

3.   A = 6   B = 8   C = 11   D = 13   E = 16   E ÷ B + A = (________)

4.   A = 3   B = 6   C = 7   D = 11   E = 30   E ÷ A + C – B = (________)

Each question uses a different code. Use the alphabet to help you work out the
answer to each question.

A B C D E F G H I J K L M N O P Q R S T U V W X Y Z

Example: If the code for **MANY** is **LZMX**, what is the code for **GREY**? (_FQDX_)

---

5.   If the code for **FOXES** is **BKTAO**, what is the code for **IMPLY**? (___________)

6.   If the code for **ZONAL** is **XSLEJ**, what is **ASSKF** the code for? (___________)

7.   If the code for **VOLT** is **WQOX**, what is **MGDR** the code for? (___________)

8.   If the code for **ENVY** is **VMEB**, what is **HVZN** the code for? (___________)

                                        38

Find the pair of letters that continues each sequence in the best way. Use the alphabet to help you.

A B C D E F G H I J K L M N O P Q R S T U V W X Y Z

Example: TU   QR   NO   KL   HI   (__EF__)

9.   RW   OT   LQ   IN   FK   (______)

10. AE   DD   GC   JB   MA   (______)

11. NI   MH   RM   QL   VQ   (______)

12. VC   TH   RL   PO   NQ   (______)

Find the number that completes the final set of numbers in the same way as the first two sets. Write your answer on the line.

Example: 7 (4) 3   10 (5) 5   15 (__11__) 4

13. 9 (13) 4   4 (7) 3   11 (______) 4

14. 3 (18) 6   2 (16) 8   6 (______) 6

15. 8 (2) 6   19 (11) 8   12 (______) 3

16. 3 (6) 4   5 (10) 4   7 (______) 2

END OF TEST

/ 16

Break time! Keep your brain ticking along by having a go at these **maths** puzzles.

A Penny Saved Is A Penny Earned

Penny wants to buy a new toy for £20 but she only has £3 in her purse.
Penny earns £5 a day by helping her parents with chores around the house.

| On Monday, Penny saves all £5.00. | On Tuesday, she spends £2.00 on an ice cream. | On Wednesday, she pays £3.50 to go bowling. |

| On Thursday, she buys a new hat for £5.00. | On Friday, Penny saves all £5.00. |

Calculate how much money Penny has in her purse at the end of each day,
then say whether she has enough money at the end of the week to buy the toy.

Monday	Tuesday	Wednesday	Thursday	Friday

Can Penny afford the toy? Circle the correct answer.   **YES / NO**

Crafty Creatures

Some of the numbers in the sums below have been replaced with creatures.
Use the first row of sums to work out which number each creature represents,
then complete the other sums by writing the missing number in each square.

You have **10 minutes** to do this test. Work as quickly and accurately as you can.

> The number codes for three of these four words are listed in a random order.
> Work out the code to answer the questions. Write your answer on the line.

WIDE   IDLE   WELD   HILL
1355   3654   2364

1.   Find the code for the word **IDLE**.   (___________)

2.   Find the code for the word **HELD**.   (___________)

3.   Find the word that has the number code **5346**. (___________)

> Find the pair of letters that continues each sequence in the best way. Use the
> alphabet to help you.
>
> A B C D E F G H I J K L M N O P Q R S T U V W X Y Z
>
> **Example:** TU   QR   NO   KL   HI   (_**EF**_)

4.   CD   GH   KL   OP   ST   (______)

5.   VQ   RN   NK   JH   FE   (______)

6.   IQ   LT   KS   NV   MU   (______)

7.   WC   RG   NH   KL   IM   (______)

Find the missing number to complete each sum. Write your answer on the line.

Example: 7 + 5 = 24 ÷ (___2___)

8.   43 – 15 = (_______)

9.   20 + 18 – 24 = (_______)

10.   14 + 22 – 18 = (_______)

11.   32 – 7 = 21 + (_______)

12.   40 ÷ 4 + 2 = 23 – (_______)

Underline the pair of letters that completes each sentence in the most sensible way. Use the alphabet to help you.

A B C D E F G H I J K L M N O P Q R S T U V W X Y Z

Example: DG is to **FE** as **RU** is to (<u>TS</u>   SR   TU   ST   US).

13.   **RE** is to **PC** as **OJ** is to   (KK   ML   MH   MK   OH).

14.   **NT** is to **PX** as **ZE** is to   (DI   AG   BH   BK   BI).

15.   **VG** is to **ZF** as **PK** is to   (TJ   WI   VJ   TH   OJ).

16.   **FW** is to **UD** as **EQ** is to (VI   VJ   WH   UL   VK).

END OF TEST

/ 16

You have **10 minutes** to do this test. Work as quickly and accurately as you can.

Find the number that completes the final set of numbers in the same way as the first two sets. Write your answer on the line.

Example: 7 (4) 3   10 (5) 5   15 (__11__) 4

---

1.   2 (10) 5   2 (14) 7   9 (________) 9

2.   5 (13) 8   10 (19) 9   6 (________) 9

3.   10 (6) 1   2 (4) 3   8 (________) 2

4.   3 (10) 2   1 (14) 6   2 (________) 2

The number codes for three of these four words are listed in a random order. Work out the code to answer the questions. Write your answer on the line.

SUMO   SORT   SOUR   MOST
3124   2435   3416

5.   Find the code for the word **SORT**.   (__________)

6.   Find the code for the word **RUST**.   (__________)

7.   Find the word that has the number code **5416**. (__________)

Each letter stands for a number. Work out the answer to each sum as a letter. Write your answer on the line.

Example: A = 1 B = 2 C = 6 D = 12 E = 10 $D \div B = ($ __C__ $)$

8.   A = 4   B = 5   C = 7   D = 21   E = 28 $A \times C = ($ ________ $)$

9.   A = 6   B = 8   C = 11   D = 12   E = 15 $D + C - E = ($ ________ $)$

10. A = 3   B = 5   C = 11   D = 17   E = 18 $E \div A + C = ($ ________ $)$

11. A = 3   B = 5   C = 8   D = 15   E = 22 $B \times A + D - C = ($ ________ $)$

Find the pair of letters that continues each sequence in the best way. Use the alphabet to help you.

A B C D E F G H I J K L M N O P Q R S T U V W X Y Z

Example: TU   QR   NO   KL   HI   (__EF__)

12. XE   TA   PW   LS   HO   (______)

13. FY   IW   LU   OS   RQ   (______)

14. YB   UD   QF   MH   IJ   (______)

15. CL   AJ   FO   DM   IR   (______)

16. WI   VJ   UL   TO   SS   (______)

END OF TEST

/ 16

You have **10 minutes** to do this test. Work as quickly and accurately as you can.

Each letter stands for a number. Work out the answer to each sum as a letter. Write your answer on the line.

Example: A = 1   B = 2   C = 6   D = 12   E = 10   D ÷ B = (___C___)

---

1.   A = 5   B = 7   C = 10   D = 11   E = 35   E ÷ B = (_________)

2.   A = 2   B = 3   C = 5   D = 12   E = 27   B × C + D = (_________)

3.   A = 3   B = 4   C = 9   D = 13   E = 23   C × A − B = (_________)

4.   A = 2   B = 5   C = 6   D = 12   E = 20   E ÷ B × A + D = (_________)

Read the information carefully, then use it to answer the question that follows.

---

5.   Raeesa, Andrew, Mia, Chris and Lucy want to see who scored the most goals for their football team. Lucy scored more goals than Chris. Raeesa scored twice as many goals as Lucy. Chris scored more goals than Andrew. Mia scored more goals than Lucy, but fewer than Raeesa.

If the statements above are true, only one of the sentences below **cannot** be true. Which one? Circle the correct letter.

A   Mia scored fewer goals than Raeesa.

B   Lucy scored the third most goals.

C   Raeesa scored the most goals.

D   Andrew scored more goals than one other person.

E   Chris scored fewer goals than Lucy.

---

6. Daniel, Rachel, Norman, Betty and Roberto all collect colourful magnets.
Rachel is the only person that doesn't have a purple magnet. Betty and Daniel
both have red magnets. Betty is the only person to have a black magnet.
Roberto and Rachel both have one green magnet and one blue magnet.
Norman also has a blue magnet.

If the statements above are true, only one of the sentences below **must** be true.
Which one? Circle the correct letter.

A   Betty and Roberto have the same coloured magnets.

B   Rachel has one green magnet and one purple magnet.

C   The red magnet is Norman's least favourite.

D   Only one person has a green magnet.

E   At least two more people own a blue magnet than a black magnet.

Find the number that continues each sequence in the best way. Write your
answer on the line.

Example: 3   6   9   12   15   (__18__)

---

7.   7   11   15   19   23   (_______)

8.   32   7   35   9   38   11   (_______)

9.   72   74   77   81   86   (_______)

10. 12   8   15   11   18   (_______)

Each question uses a different code. Use the alphabet to help you work out the answer to each question.

A B C D E F G H I J K L M N O P Q R S T U V W X Y Z

Example: If the code for **MANY** is **LZMX**, what is the code for **GREY**? (<u>FQDX</u>)

11.   If the code for **WOULD** is **ZRXOG**, what is **KDXQW** the code for? (___________)

12.   If the code for **STAR** is **XPFN**, what is the code for **MOLE**? (___________)

13.   If the code for **MENU** is **NEMS**, what is the code for **RUIN**? (___________)

14.   If the code for **FONT** is **ULMG**, what is **XZKV** the code for? (___________)

END OF TEST

/ 14

10

You have **10 minutes** to do this test. Work as quickly and accurately as you can.

> Each question uses a different code. Use the alphabet to help you work out the answer to each question.
>
> A B C D E F G H I J K L M N O P Q R S T U V W X Y Z
>
> **Example:** If the code for **MANY** is **LZMX**, what is the code for **GREY**? (<u>FQDX</u>)

1.   If the code for **BLANK** is **GQFSP**, what is the code for **AMUSE**?   (_____________)

2.   If the code for **GLOVE** is **DJLTB**, what is **TFFQH** the code for?   (_____________)

3.   If the code for **CHASM** is **DJDWR**, what is **DQPIY** the code for?   (_____________)

4.   If the code for **NOTE** is **MLGV**, what is **IRMT** the code for?   (_____________)

> Find the missing number to complete each sum. Write your answer on the line.
>
> **Example:** $7 + 5 = 24 \div ($ <u> 2 </u> $)$

5. $30 - 14 = ($ ________ $)$

6. $3 \times 4 + 13 = ($ ________ $)$

7. $6 + 26 = 40 - ($ ________ $)$

8. $25 \div 5 + 7 = 2 \times ($ ________ $)$

9.   **YB** is to **AD** as **QH** is to (SJ   RM   TM   TJ   SI).

10.   **JD** is to **OF** as **FK** is to   (MK   KM   LM   JO   KN).

11.   **TY** is to **YX** as **RG** is to   (WI   WF   SE   WE   XD).

12.   **YK** is to **BP** as **JS** is to   (QF   RI   QJ   QH   QI).

13.   32   53   42   43   52   33   (______)

14.   11   18   25   32   39   (______)

15.   54   57   61   66   72   (______)

16.   15   23   22   30   29   (______)

END OF TEST

/ 16

These puzzles are a superb way to practise your **logic** and **sequencing** skills.

Suzie's Seashells

Suzie collects seashells, but she is not very good at remembering how many she has of each type. Use the facts below to fill in the table for her.

- She has two cockles.

- She has four fewer nutmegs than scallops.

- She has more scallops than any other type of seashell.

- She has six more scallops than cockles.

- She has more conches than cockles, but more nutmegs than conches.

	Cockles	Nutmegs	Scallops	Conches
Number owned				

Sneaky Spy

Agent Alex has received a coded message from a fellow spy containing the location of their next mission. Fill in the gaps in each sequence, then unscramble the missing letters to reveal the location. Each sequence uses a different pattern.

A B C D E F G H I J K L M N O P Q R S T U V W X Y Z

N	K	H	___	B
ABD	F___I	KL___	PQS
B	EF	I___K	NOPQ
XD	___H	R___	OP	LT

The location of the next mission is the ________________ .

You have **10 minutes** to do this test. Work as quickly and accurately as you can.

Each letter stands for a number. Work out the answer to each sum as a letter.
Write your answer on the line.

Example: A = 1 B = 2 C = 6 D = 12 E = 10   D ÷ B = (___C___)

---

1.   A = 4   B = 8   C = 11 D = 14 E = 19   B + C = (________)

2.   A = 4   B = 6   C = 11 D = 13 E = 14   D + A − B = (________)

3.   A = 2   B = 3   C = 7   D = 19 E = 21   B × C − A = (________)

4.   A = 3   B = 5   C = 6   D = 7   E = 20   E ÷ B + C − A = (________)

Read the information carefully, then use it to answer the question that follows.

---

5.   Tim, Chloe, Karl, Anele and Mark are lining up according to their age, with
the oldest at the front. Mark is not at the front of the line. Chloe is standing
behind Mark but in front of Anele. Tim is closer to the back of the line than
Chloe. Karl is closer to the front of the line than Chloe.

If the statements above are true, only one of the sentences below **must** be true.
Which one? Circle the correct letter.

A   Chloe is at the back of the line.

B   Anele is at the front of the line.

C   Mark is standing behind Karl.

D   Anele is standing behind Tim.

E   Tim is standing in front of Mark.

6. Stacey, Ben, Uzair, Lizzie and Peter all take fruit to school. Everyone takes a banana except for Stacey and Uzair. Stacey and Peter both take an orange and a kiwi. Lizzie also takes a kiwi. Ben and Uzair both take some mango, but Uzair also takes strawberries. No one takes any other fruit.

If the statements above are true, only one of the sentences below **must** be true. Which one? Circle the correct letter.

A   Three people take both a banana and some mango to school.

B   Peter takes one more type of fruit to school than Lizzie.

C   Two people take strawberries to school.

D   Ben and Lizzie take exactly the same types of fruit to school.

E   No one likes raspberries.

The number codes for three of these four words are listed in a random order. Work out the code to answer the questions. Write your answer on the line.

LONE   NODE   LEND   ROLE

5612   3652   5214

7.   Find the code for the word **NODE**.   (___________)

8.   Find the code for the word **REDO**.   (___________)

9.   Find the word that has the number code **5634**. (___________)

Find the number that continues each sequence in the best way. Write your answer on the line.

Example: 3   6   9   12   15   (__18__)

10. 38   33   28   23   18   (_______)

11. 65   64   64   65   67   (_______)

12. 22   51   17   57   12   63   (_______)

13. 7   11   21   25   35   (_______)

14. 23   20   19   30   15   40   (_______)

END OF TEST

/ 14

You have **10 minutes** to do this test. Work as quickly and accurately as you can.

Find the number that completes the final set of numbers in the same way as the first two sets. Write your answer on the line.

Example: 7 (4) 3   10 (5) 5   15 (___11___) 4

---

1.   10 (4) 6   9 (2) 7   8 (_______) 3

2.   8 (4) 2   20 (2) 10   27 (_______) 9

3.   6 (5) 2   4 (7) 5   4 (_______) 3

4.   6 (8) 10   2 (5) 8   3 (_______) 5

Underline the pair of letters that completes each sentence in the most sensible way. Use the alphabet to help you.

A B C D E F G H I J K L M N O P Q R S T U V W X Y Z

Example: DG is to **FE** as **RU** is to (TS   SR   TU   ST   US).

---

5.   **GF** is to **LK** as **TN** is to (ZS   YT   YR   YS   XU).

6.   **FH** is to **HM** as **TB** is to (VG   UE   VE   WF   VD).

7.   **ES** is to **AV** as **JA** is to   (EC   FB   DD   FD   FF).

8.   **BO** is to **YL** as **GP** is to (TK   SL   TJ   SJ   TM).

9. $21 + 26 = ($ _______ $)$

10. $8 \times 2 - 9 = ($ _______ $)$

11. $6 + 5 = 44 \div ($ _______ $)$

12. $22 \div 2 + 3 = 7 + ($ _______ $)$

13. Aaron, Marijke, Nathan, Robyn and Duncan are raising money for charity by doing a walkathon. Nathan manages to walk 35 miles. Aaron walks further than Marijke, but not as far as Nathan. Marijke walks 10 miles further than Duncan. Duncan walks the same distance as Robyn.

If the statements above are true, only one of the sentences below **must** be true. Which one? Circle the correct letter.

A Robyn and Marijke walk the same distance.

B Aaron doesn't like walking as much as Marijke.

C Nathan walks the furthest distance.

D Duncan and Robyn walk further than two other people.

E Aaron walks 35 miles.

14. Tammy, Max, Tshepo, Eva and Kieran are discussing how much money they
have saved. Max has saved more money than Eva. Kieran has managed to
save £20. Tshepo has saved more money than Kieran, but £5 less than Eva.
Tammy has not saved the least amount of money.

If the statements above are true, only one of the sentences below **cannot** be true.
Which one? Circle the correct letter.

A   Max and Tshepo both saved the same amount of money.

B   Tammy has saved more money than Kieran.

C   Tshepo has saved the third most amount of money.

D   Eva has saved the second most amount of money.

E   Max prefers saving money rather than spending it.

END OF TEST

/ 14

Test 22

You have **10 minutes** to do this test. Work as quickly and accurately as you can.

Find the pair of letters that continues each sequence in the best way. Use the alphabet to help you.

A B C D E F G H I J K L M N O P Q R S T U V W X Y Z

Example: TU   QR   NO   KL   HI   (__EF__)

---

1.   BE   FI   JM   NQ   RU   (______)

2.   TE   RH   PK   NN   LQ   (______)

3.   PF   ME   JD   GC   DB   (______)

4.   NU   LS   IP   GN   DK   (______)

5.   VH   RI   SI   OH   PF   (______)

Each letter stands for a number. Work out the answer to each sum as a letter. Write your answer on the line.

Example: A = 1   B = 2   C = 6   D = 12   E = 10   D ÷ B = (__C__)

---

6.   A = 3   B = 9   C = 12   D = 18   E = 27   B × A = (________)

7.   A = 4   B = 8   C = 9   D = 13   E = 14   B + C − A = (________)

8.   A = 2   B = 6   C = 8   D = 13   E = 20   B × A + C = (________)

9.   A = 3   B = 6   C = 8   D = 10   E = 12   E ÷ A + D − C = (________)

      57

The number codes for three of these four words are listed in a random order.
Work out the code to answer the questions. Write your answer on the line.

FAST   FEAT   TAME   FATE
6324   5316   5436

10.   Find the code for the word **FEAT**.   (_________)

11.   Find the code for the word **STEM**.   (_________)

12.   Find the word that has the number code **1354**. (_________)

Each question uses a different code. Use the alphabet to help you work out the
answer to each question.

A B C D E F G H I J K L M N O P Q R S T U V W X Y Z

Example: If the code for **MANY** is **LZMX**, what is the code for **GREY**? (FQDX)

13.   If the code for **EQUIP** is **AMQEL**, what is **OEJCA** the code for? (_________)

14.   If the code for **NIGHT** is **OGHFU**, what is the code for **BUILT**? (_________)

15.   If the code for **DOOR** is **GQPR**, what is **ZCST** the code for? (_________)

16.   If the code for **BUMP** is **YFNK**, what is the code for **BAND**? (_________)

END OF TEST

/ 16

You have **10 minutes** to do this test. Work as quickly and accurately as you can.

Find the number that completes the final set of numbers in the same way as the first two sets. Write your answer on the line.

Example: 7 (4) 3   10 (5) 5   15 (__11__) 4

---

1.   2 (18) 9   3 (9) 3   5 (_______) 9

2.   6 (10) 4   11 (16) 5   6 (_______) 7

3.   15 (6) 3   30 (11) 3   12 (_______) 2

4.   9 (4) 5   8 (5) 3   20 (_______) 4

Underline the pair of letters that completes each sentence in the most sensible way. Use the alphabet to help you.

A B C D E F G H I J K L M N O P Q R S T U V W X Y Z

Example: **DG** is to **FE** as **RU** is to (TS   SR   TU   ST   US).

---

5.   **LM** is to **IJ** as **WU** is to (RT   TP   TS   TR   TT).

6.   **DB** is to **IE** as **LE** is to   (SF   SK   QK   QH   QJ).

7.   **RV** is to **TR** as **MX** is to (RW   RU   NT   OT   OR).

8.   **QK** is to **JP** as **DF** is to   (WT   WS   WU   YS   VW).

Find the missing number to complete each sum. Write your answer on the line.

Example: $7 + 5 = 24 \div ($ ___2___ $)$

9. $23 + 15 = ($ _______ $)$

10. $16 + 17 - 22 = ($ _______ $)$

11. $7 \times 3 = 4 + ($ _______ $)$

12. $18 \div 9 + 8 = 16 - ($ _______ $)$

Find the pair of letters that continues each sequence in the best way. Use the alphabet to help you.

A B C D E F G H I J K L M N O P Q R S T U V W X Y Z

Example: TU   QR   NO   KL   HI   (___EF___)

13. EC   HF   KI   NL   QO   (______)

14. LV   JR   HN   FJ   DF   (______)

15. JZ   KU   MS   NN   PL   (______)

16. UG   PH   NJ   IM   GQ   (______)

END OF TEST

/ 16

Phew, have a break! This puzzle page will test your **coding** and **sequencing** skills.

Chef Charlotte's Code

Chef Charlotte only trusts cooks with excellent logic skills, so every cook she works with has to crack a secret code that has two alternating sequences. Solve the code, then read the message to find out if Chef Charlotte will hire you.

Code	A	B	C	D	E	F	G	H	I	J	K	L	M
Solution	E	Z	G	B	I	D							

N	O	P	Q	R	S	T	U	V	W	X	Y	Z

C K K F   S K T G   —   U K Q ' T A

___ ___ ___ ___   ___ ___ ___ ___   —   ___ ___ ___ ' ___

K P   V J A   V A W I !

___ ___   ___ ___ ___   ___ ___ ___ ___ !

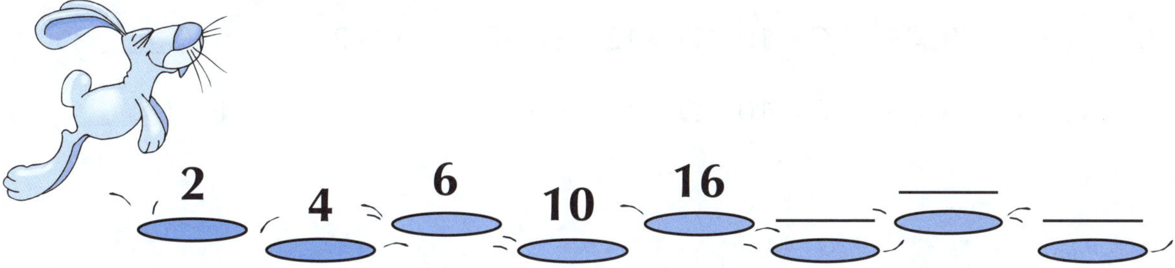

Hopping Hero

Bella the Bunny wants to hop across Swift Stream using the number stones. However, the stones will disappear unless all the numbers in the sequence are filled in correctly. Fill in each number to help Bella cross Swift Stream.

2   4   6   10   16   ___

You have **10 minutes** to do this test. Work as quickly and accurately as you can.

The number codes for three of these four words are listed in a random order. Work out the code to answer the questions. Write your answer on the line.

SUCH   HUTS   THUS   CATS
2356   6312   1456

1.   Find the code for the word **SUCH**.   (__________)

2.   Find the code for the word **CAST**.   (__________)

3.   Find the word that has the number code **6235**. (__________)

Each letter stands for a number. Work out the answer to each sum as a letter. Write your answer on the line.

Example: A = 1 B = 2 C = 6 D = 12 E = 10 $D \div B = ($ ___C___ $)$

4.   A = 4   B = 17   C = 21   D = 23   E = 22 $B + A = ($ ________ $)$

5.   A = 5   B = 8   C = 11   D = 15   E = 20 $E \div A + C = ($ ________ $)$

6.   A = 3   B = 5   C = 6   D = 8   E = 11 $D + C - E = ($ ________ $)$

7.   A = 3   B = 5   C = 10   D = 12   E = 40 $E \div B - A = ($ ________ $)$

8.   A = 2   B = 6   C = 10   D = 11   E = 13 $A \times B + D - E = ($ ________ $)$

          62

Find the number that completes the final set of numbers in the same way as the first two sets. Write your answer on the line.

Example: 7 (4) 3   10 (5) 5   15 (__11__) 4

9.   14 (2) 7   15 (3) 5   18 (_______) 6

10.   10 (17) 7   8 (14) 6   10 (_______) 10

11.   7 (3) 1   10 (4) 2   6 (_______) 4

12.   30 (2) 10   12 (3) 3   25 (_______) 5

Underline the pair of letters that completes each sentence in the most sensible way. Use the alphabet to help you.

A B C D E F G H I J K L M N O P Q R S T U V W X Y Z

Example: DG is to **FE** as **RU** is to (<u>TS</u>   SR   TU   ST   US).

13.   **MF** is to **PI** as **OW** is to (SY   RX   RY   RZ   RB).

14.   **DM** is to **AK** as **JC** is to (IA   FZ   GZ   GA   GB).

15.   **PB** is to **KF** as **IM** is to   (DQ   DR   BS   CS   BQ).

16.   **IM** is to **RN** as **TW** is to (GD   GB   EB   GF   GE).

END OF TEST

/ 16

🕙 **10**

You have **10 minutes** to do this test. Work as quickly and accurately as you can.

Find the pair of letters that continues each sequence in the best way. Use the alphabet to help you.

A B C D E F G H I J K L M N O P Q R S T U V W X Y Z

Example: TU   QR   NO   KL   HI   (__EF__)

---

1.   NO   MT   LY   KD   JI   (______)

2.   IX   LT   OP   RL   UH   (______)

3.   BY   FT   CU   GP   DQ   (______)

4.   LJ   IO   KS   HV   JX   (______)

Find the missing number to complete each sum. Write your answer on the line.

Example: $7 + 5 = 24 \div (\underline{\quad 2 \quad})$

---

5. $16 \div 4 = (\underline{\qquad})$

6. $110 \div 10 = 17 - (\underline{\qquad})$

7. $3 \times 6 + 9 = (\underline{\qquad})$

8. $4 + 16 - 11 = 3 \times (\underline{\qquad})$

Each question uses a different code. Use the alphabet to help you work out the answer to each question.

A B C D E F G H I J K L M N O P Q R S T U V W X Y Z

Example: If the code for **MANY** is **LZMX**, what is the code for **GREY**? (<u>FQDX</u>)

9.   If the code for **METAL** is **RJYFQ**, what is **LWZSY** the code for? (____________)

10.   If the code for **JADE** is **NDHH**, what is the code for **COLD**? (____________)

11.   If the code for **SHAKE** is **RHBMH**, what is **RTPTP** the code for? (____________)

12.   If the code for **WISH** is **DRHS**, what is the code for **TOMB**? (____________)

Read the information carefully, then use it to answer the question that follows.

13.   James, Paula, Stuart, Bea and David are seeing who can balance on one leg for the longest time. James keeps his balance for five minutes. Paula keeps her balance for twice as long as James, but for less time than Bea. Stuart keeps his balance for longer than Paula, but for less time than David. David does not balance on one leg for the longest time.

If the statements above are true, only one of the sentences below **cannot** be true. Which one? Circle the correct letter.

A   David balances on one leg for longer than James.

B   James balances on one leg for the third longest time.

C   Bea has more practice at balancing on one leg than David.

D   James balances on one leg for less time than Stuart.

E   Paula balances on one leg for less time than Stuart.

14. Katherine, Aubrey, Caroline, Michael and Jacqui played a round of
'Pass the Parcel'. Katherine was the only person who wasn't passed the parcel
during the round. Jacqui was the third person to have the parcel. Aubrey was
not the second person to have the parcel. Aubrey passed the parcel to Michael.
Katherine passed the parcel to Caroline. Everyone only held the parcel once.

If the statements above are true, only one of the sentences below **must** be true.
Which one? Circle the correct letter.

A   Aubrey passed the parcel to Katherine.

B   Jacqui's favourite game is 'Pass the Parcel'.

C   Caroline was the second person to hold the parcel.

D   Aubrey received the parcel from Michael.

E   Michael was the second to last person to receive the parcel.

END OF TEST

/ 14

You have **10 minutes** to do this test. Work as quickly and accurately as you can.

> Find the number that continues each sequence in the best way. Write your answer on the line.
>
> **Example:** 3   6   9   12   15   (__18__)

1.   5   12   19   26   33   (_______)

2.   54   29   58   35   62   41   (_______)

3.   25   26   29   34   41   (_______)

4.   10   20   12   22   14   (_______)

5.   11   6   14   9   17   (_______)

> Underline the pair of letters that completes each sentence in the most sensible way. Use the alphabet to help you.
>
> A B C D E F G H I J K L M N O P Q R S T U V W X Y Z
>
> **Example:** **DG** is to **FE** as **RU** is to (<u>TS</u>   SR   TU   ST   US).

6.   **DR** is to **BP** as **UH** is to (SD   SF   SI   PF   VE).

7.   **GT** is to **DP** as **PX** is to (LS   NS   MU   LT   MT).

8.   **TF** is to **RK** as **ON** is to (PV   MS   MQ   LS   JV).

9.   **XU** is to **CF** as **WR** is to (DI   EG   DJ   CG   DH).

BIND   **BEDS**   **SEND**   **DIES**
5412   6435   2135

10.   Find the code for the word **SEND**.   (__________)

11.   Find the code for the word **NIBS**.   (__________)

12.   Find the word that has the number code **5431**.   (__________)

13.   A = 3   B = 4   C = 8   D = 24   E = 27 $A \times C$ = (________)

14.   A = 3   B = 6   C = 9   D = 11   E = 14 $B + D - E$ = (________)

15.   A = 3   B = 6   C = 9   D = 10   E = 15 $B \times A - E$ = (________)

16.   A = 3   B = 8   C = 9   D = 10   E = 20 $E \div D + C - A$ = (________)

END OF TEST

/ 16

You have **10 minutes** to do this test. Work as quickly and accurately as you can.

Each question uses a different code. Use the alphabet to help you work out the answer to each question.

A B C D E F G H I J K L M N O P Q R S T U V W X Y Z

Example: If the code for **MANY** is **LZMX**, what is the code for **GREY**? (<u>FQDX</u>)

---

1. If the code for **MARSH** is **PDUVK**, what is the code for **VIDEO**? (___________)

2. If the code for **EMPTY** is **FRQYZ**, what is the code for **QUICK**? (___________)

3. If the code for **GAWK** is **HAVI**, what is **IOOC** the code for? (___________)

4. If the code for **VOTE** is **ELGV**, what is the code for **HARP**? (___________)

Read the information carefully, then use it to answer the question that follows.

---

5. Danielle, George, Rebecca, Sean and Zinhle all sell frisbees at the beach. Zinhle sells four more frisbees than Rebecca. Sean sells more frisbees than Rebecca but fewer frisbees than Zinhle. George does not sell the fewest frisbees. Danielle sells fewer frisbees than Rebecca.

If the statements above are true, only one of the sentences below **must** be true. Which one? Circle the correct letter.

A Zinhle sells the fewest frisbees.

B Rebecca sells four more frisbees than Zinhle.

C George sells more frisbees than Sean.

D Sean sells the second largest number of frisbees.

E Zinhle sells more frisbees than Danielle.

6.   Skye, Caitlin, Busisiwe, Amy and Millie met each other at their favourite cafe.
Millie arrived 5 minutes before Amy. Busisiwe arrived 10 minutes after Millie.
Skye arrived after Amy. Caitlin arrived after Skye, but before Busisiwe.

If the statements above are true, only one of the sentences below **must** be true.
Which one? Circle the correct letter.

A   Skye was the second person to arrive.

B   Caitlin arrived last.

C   Millie was the third person to arrive.

D   Busisiwe arrived five minutes after Amy.

E   Skye and Busisiwe arrived at the same time.

Find the number that continues each sequence in the best way. Write your
answer on the line.

Example: 3   6   9   12   15   (__18__)

---

7.   64   32   16   8   4   (_______)

8.   57   52   48   45   43   (_______)

9.   47   23   51   13   55   3   (_______)

10.   21   16   20   15   19   (_______)

Example: $7 + 5 = 24 \div (\underline{\quad 2 \quad})$

11. $4 \times 7 = (\underline{\quad\quad\quad})$

12. $10 \times 4 - 25 = (\underline{\quad\quad\quad})$

13. $45 - 13 = 25 + (\underline{\quad\quad\quad})$

14. $11 \times 5 - 10 = 41 + (\underline{\quad\quad\quad})$

END OF TEST

/ 14

It's puzzle time again! This page is about using your **logic** and **related number** skills.

Nkosi's Shapes

Nkosi is trying to complete the puzzle below, but he is stuck. Complete the grid so that every row and column contains four different shapes. You can only use the shapes which are already in the grid.

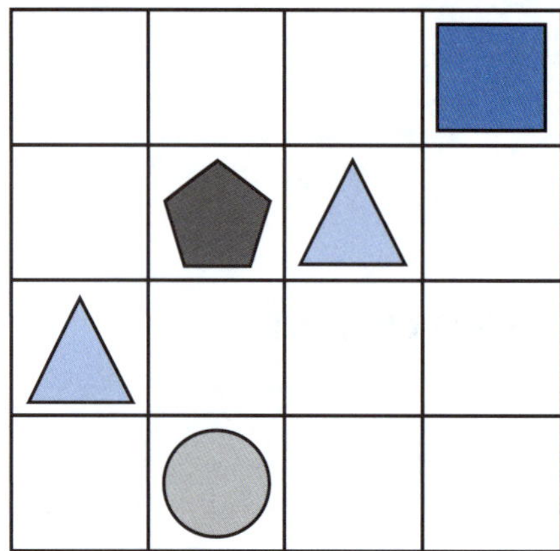

Esmerelda's Treasure

Esmerelda the Explorer has one clue left to solve in her hunt for lost treasure. To solve the final clue, she must complete a secret combination of numbers.

Follow the instructions below to help her work out the combination. Write the missing numbers in each box.

Each side of the square should add up to 17.

The total of the white boxes is 22.

The blue boxes should add up to 24.

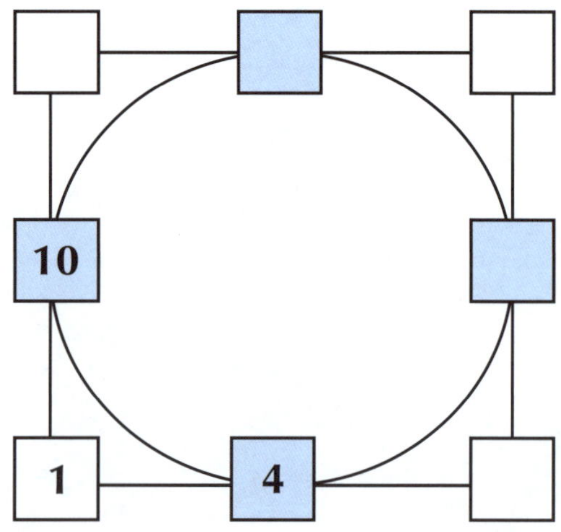

You have **10 minutes** to do this test. Work as quickly and accurately as you can.

Find the number that completes the final set of numbers in the same way as the first two sets. Write your answer on the line.

Example: 7 (4) 3   10 (5) 5   15 (__11__) 4

1.   4 (3) 1   8 (5) 3   18 (_______) 7

2.   4 (16) 4   5 (35) 7   2 (_______) 11

3.   3 (11) 4   2 (14) 6   3 (_______) 5

4.   10 (14) 5   9 (12) 4   2 (_______) 9

Underline the pair of letters that completes each sentence in the most sensible way. Use the alphabet to help you.

A B C D E F G H I J K L M N O P Q R S T U V W X Y Z

Example: DG is to **FE** as **RU** is to (<u>TS</u>   SR   TU   ST   US).

5.   **TO** is to **OJ** as **IQ** is to   (DL   DN   FI   DJ   BL).

6.   **RF** is to **MB** as **BL** is to   (WH   XH   XF   WG   VG).

7.   **EP** is to **JM** as **JH** is to   (OF   PE   OE   PH   NF).

8.   **ZE** is to **AV** as **LG** is to   (MT   PU   OS   PS   OT).

Each letter stands for a number. Work out the answer to each sum as a letter. Write your answer on the line.

Example: A = 1   B = 2   C = 6   D = 12   E = 10   D ÷ B = (___C___)

9.   A = 9   B = 13   C = 14   D = 27   E = 29   C + B = (_________)

10.   A = 3   B = 7   C = 13   D = 16   E = 21   E ÷ B + C = (_________)

11.   A = 2   B = 3   C = 6   D = 12   E = 16   A × C + B − D = (_________)

12.   A = 2   B = 3   C = 10   D = 12   E = 27   C ÷ A × B + D = (_________)

Find the pair of letters that continues each sequence in the best way. Use the alphabet to help you.

A B C D E F G H I J K L M N O P Q R S T U V W X Y Z

Example: TU   QR   NO   KL   HI   (___EF___)

13.   QO   LQ   GS   BU   WW   (_______)

14.   VB   SC   PD   ME   JF   (_______)

15.   TC   PA   OD   KB   JE   (_______)

16.   XF   WG   UI   RJ   NL   (_______)

END OF TEST

/ 16

10

You have **10 minutes** to do this test. Work as quickly and accurately as you can.

Find the pair of letters that continues each sequence in the best way. Use the alphabet to help you.

A B C D E F G H I J K L M N O P Q R S T U V W X Y Z

Example: TU   QR   NO   KL   HI   (__EF__)

---

1.   FM   GR   HW   IB   JG   (______)

2.   GU   JV   MW   PX   SY   (______)

3.   MO   IP   NK   JL   OG   (______)

4.   ML   NK   OK   PL   QN   (______)

The number codes for three of these four words are listed in a random order. Work out the code to answer the questions. Write your answer on the line.

PERK   RIPE   KITE   TIRE
2351   6453   5423

5.   Find the code for the word **KITE**.   (__________)

6.   Find the code for the word **TRIP**.   (__________)

7.   Find the word that has the number code **2435**. (__________)

Underline the pair of letters that completes each sentence in the most sensible way. Use the alphabet to help you.

A B C D E F G H I J K L M N O P Q R S T U V W X Y Z

Example: DG is to **FE** as **RU** is to (<u>TS</u> SR TU ST US).

8. **EA** is to **AW** as **TX** is to (PR RW PS OT PT).

9. **RI** is to **OD** as **YM** is to (VG UH TH TJ VH).

10. **PW** is to **SU** as **GM** is to (GK JK LJ JH MN).

11. **KD** is to **PW** as **NJ** is to (NO KQ MQ MP NS).

Each letter stands for a number. Work out the answer to each sum as a letter. Write your answer on the line.

Example: A = 1 B = 2 C = 6 D = 12 E = 10   D ÷ B = (___C___)

12. A = 3   B = 6   C = 18   D = 21   E = 24   B × A = (_________)

13. A = 5   B = 7   C = 10   D = 11   E = 14   C + D − E = (________)

14. A = 5   B = 7   C = 9   D = 11   E = 14   A + D − B = (________)

15. A = 3   B = 6   C = 7   D = 11   E = 16   A × C + B − D = (________)

16. A = 3   B = 4   C = 6   D = 15   E = 19   B × A + C − D = (________)

END OF TEST

/ 16

You have **10 minutes** to do this test. Work as quickly and accurately as you can.

Each question uses a different code. Use the alphabet to help you work out the answer to each question.

A B C D E F G H I J K L M N O P Q R S T U V W X Y Z

Example: If the code for **MANY** is **LZMX**, what is the code for **GREY**? (<u>FQDX</u>)

1. If the code for **CLOSE** is **HOTVJ**, what is the code for **TIGER**? (_____________)

2. If the code for **DATA** is **ECWE**, what is **TQLP** the code for? (_____________)

3. If the code for **PRIME** is **KIRNV**, what is the code for **LATER**? (_____________)

4. If the code for **CORK** is **ASPO**, what is **QEJI** the code for? (_____________)

Find the missing number to complete each sum. Write your answer on the line.

Example: $7 + 5 = 24 ÷ ($ <u>2</u> $)$

5. $6 × 4 - 5 = ($ _______ $)$

6. $36 ÷ 6 = 2 + ($ _______ $)$

7. $13 + 17 = 6 × ($ _______ $)$

8. $33 ÷ 3 + 4 = 3 × ($ _______ $)$

Find the pair of letters that continues each sequence in the best way. Use the alphabet to help you.

A B C D E F G H I J K L M N O P Q R S T U V W X Y Z

Example: TU   QR   NO   KL   HI   (__EF__)

9.   SM   TP   US   VV   WY   (______)

10. XW   US   RO   OK   LG   (______)

11. BO   AJ   DM   CH   FK   (______)

12. IB   GC   EG   CH   AL   (______)

Find the number that completes the final set of numbers in the same way as the first two sets. Write your answer on the line.

Example: 7 (4) 3   10 (5) 5   15 (__11__) 4

13.   2 (10) 8   3 (12) 9   7 (______) 8

14.   4 (16) 4   2 (20) 10   5 (______) 6

15.   4 (9) 4   6 (10) 3   5 (______) 9

16.   50 (4) 10   12 (2) 4   8 (______) 2

END OF TEST

/ 16

10

You have **10 minutes** to do this test. Work as quickly and accurately as you can.

Find the missing number to complete each sum. Write your answer on the line.

Example: $7 + 5 = 24 \div (\underline{\quad 2 \quad})$

---

1. $8 \times 3 = 30 - (\underline{\qquad})$

2. $24 \div 4 = 16 - (\underline{\qquad})$

3. $35 \div 5 - 3 = (\underline{\qquad})$

4. $9 \times 3 + 3 = 37 - (\underline{\qquad})$

Find the number that continues each sequence in the best way. Write your answer on the line.

Example: 3   6   9   12   15 $(\underline{\quad 18 \quad})$

---

5.   3   6   12   24   48 $(\underline{\qquad})$

6.   45   44   42   39   35 $(\underline{\qquad})$

7.   32   49   27   45   22   41 $(\underline{\qquad})$

8.   13   17   11   15   9 $(\underline{\qquad})$

---

9. Thomas, Hazel, Cameron, Samiha and Liam timed how long they slept for last night. Cameron slept for less time than Hazel, but for more time than Samiha. Liam slept for two hours longer than Thomas. Hazel and Thomas both slept for 12 hours.

If the statements above are true, only one of the sentences below **must** be true. Which one? Circle the correct letter.

A Thomas slept for less time than Samiha.

B Cameron was asleep for the shortest time.

C Samiha slept for more time than Liam.

D Hazel and Thomas were asleep for longer than two other people.

E Liam slept for six hours.

10. Sian, Jamaal, Hannah, Miles and Abby are on a treasure hunt to find gold coins. Miles finds fewer coins than Jamaal. Abby finds half as many coins as Sian, but more coins than Hannah. Jamaal finds fewer coins than Abby, but more coins than Hannah. Hannah ends the hunt with more coins than Miles.

If the statements above are true, only one of the sentences below **must** be true. Which one? Circle the correct letter.

A Abby finds fewer coins than Miles.

B Hannah finds twice as many coins as Sian.

C Miles finds the fewest coins.

D Jamaal finds more coins than Sian.

E Hannah finds more coins than two other people.

11. If the code for **FELT** is **HCNR**, what is **GVCK** the code for? (_____________)

12. If the code for **PARTY** is **QCSVZ**, what is **CNFPE** the code for? (_____________)

13. If the code for **GUILT** is **DTJOY**, what is the code for **LEDGE**? (_____________)

14. If the code for **WARP** is **DZIK**, what is the code for **PICK**? (_____________)

END OF TEST

/ 14

Just one more page! These puzzles will give your **logic** and **coding** skills a work out.

Television Time

Travis, Tasmeen, Tamara and Teo love watching television.
Use the facts below to work out who watches the most television.

- Tamara watches half the amount of television that Teo does.

- Travis watches double the amount of television that Tasmeen does.

- Teo watches television between 19:00 and 20:30.

- Tasmeen watches television for 15 minutes longer than Tamara.

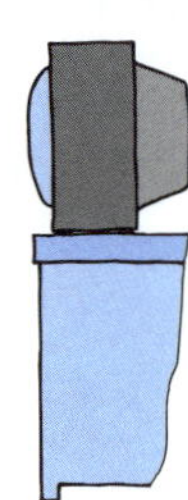

Who watches the most television? ___________________

Captain Codey's Conundrum

Captain Codey must visit five different towns to collect some clues for a secret mission. However, the names of these towns have been disguised. He has worked out that one town, known as **? # ! £ $ @ £**, is really called **Laskirk**. Match the other disguised names to the towns' real names.

% # ? ? + $ *	**Silkett**
@ = ! & ! # %	**Walltin**
% & ! % $? £	**Rosesaw**
! $? £ & + +	**Weswilk**

Test 1 — pages 2-4

1.   47
Add 8 each time.

2.   28
The number added decreases by 1 each time:
+5, +4, +3, +2, +1.

3.   55
There are two sequences which alternate. In the first sequence,
add 2 each time. In the second sequence, multiply by 2 each time.

4.   27
The numbers follow the sequence +6, −3, +6, −3, +6.

5.   PAINT
To get from the code to the word, move each letter back 2.

6.   MUCH
To get from the code to the word, move the letters in the sequence
−3, +4, −3, +4.

7.   MENP
To get from the word to the code, move the letters in the sequence
+5, +4, +5, +4.

8.   MCPF
To get from the word to the code, move the letters in the sequence
+1, +2, +3, +4.

9.   A
$18 \div 9 = 2, A = 2$

10.   B
$9 + 10 - 14 = 5, B = 5$

11.   C
$28 \div 7 + 2 = 6, C = 6$

12.   E
$25 \div 5 \times 4 + 6 = 26, E = 26$

13.   C
Nabeel had the highest throw and Adam threw the ball higher than
Saiesha. Saiesha threw the ball higher than Tyron, who threw the
ball higher than Julian. Therefore, two people threw the ball higher
than Saiesha and two people threw the ball lower than her, so she
had the third highest throw.

14.   C
Dean and Matt are the only two who do not have maths homework,
so Alisa has maths homework. Alisa also has homework for
geography and English. Dean only has homework for history.
Therefore Alisa has homework for two subjects more than Dean.

Test 2 — pages 5-6

1.   30
Subtract 4 each time.

2.   47
The number subtracted increases by 1 each time:
−1, −2, −3, −4, −5

3.   3
The number is halved each time.

4.   9
There are two sequences which alternate. In the first sequence,
subtract 3 each time. In the second sequence, add 2 each time.

5.   17
The numbers follow the sequence −3, +4, −3, +4, −3.

6.   1325
H = 1, E = 3, A = 2, L = 5

7.   4253
P = 4, A = 2, L = 5, E = 3

8.   LAPS
L = 5, A = 2, P = 4, S = 6

9.   B
$13 - 5 = 8, B = 8$

10.   C
$16 \div 4 + 5 = 9, C = 9$

11.   C
$10 \times 2 - 11 = 9, C = 9$

12.   B
$20 \div 4 + 7 - 6 = 6, B = 6$

13.   GSEWX
To get from the word to the code, move each letter forward 4.

14.   HOIST
To get from the code to the word, move the letters in the sequence
−5, +4, −5, +4, −5.

15.   KNFUP
To get from the word to the code, move the letters in the sequence
+5, +2, +5, +2, +5.

16.   BRFY
To get from the word to the code, move the letters in the sequence
−1, 0, +1, +2.

Test 3 — pages 7-8

1. 48
$8 \times 6 = 48$

2. 11
$9 \div 3 + 8 = 11$

3. 7
$7 \times 2 = 14, 14 = 21 - 17$

4. 5
$19 - 14 = 5, 5 = 25 \div 5$

5. TX
The first letter in the pair moves forward 1 letter.
The second letter in the pair moves forward 4 letters.

6. KO
The first letter in the pair moves back 4 letters.
The second letter in the pair moves back 5 letters.

7. EH
The first letter in the pair moves back 3 letters.
The second letter in the pair moves forward 5 letters.

8. VX
TM and GN are mirror pairs, where the two letters are an equal
distance from the centre of the alphabet. The answer will be the
mirror pairs for E and C, which are V and X.

9. KN
Each letter in the pair moves back 5 letters each time.

10. QV
The first letter in the pair moves forward 1 letter each time.
The second letter in the pair moves forward 3 letters each time.

11. AX
Each letter in the pair moves forward 5 letters
and then forward 3 letters alternately.

12. DO
The first letter in the pair moves forward 3 letters then back
5 letters alternately. The second letter in the pair moves
forward 4 letters then forward 5 letters alternately.

13. 4
Divide the first number by the third number.

14. 28
Multiply the two outside numbers together.

15. 6
Multiply the third number by 2, then add the first number.

16. 8
Subtract the third number from the first number,
then multiply by 2.

Puzzles 1 — page 9

Confusing Kassaqr
To get from the code to the word, move the vowels forward to the
vowel before and the consonants forward to the consonant before.
The note says: **Dear Emma, I won the game!**

Wriggling Wes
There are four of Book A, so $4 \times 2 = 8$ minutes.
There are four of Book B, so $4 \times 3 = 12$ minutes.
There are four of Book C, so $4 \times 4 = 16$ minutes.
Wesley takes four breaks, so $4 \times 5 = 20$ minutes.
$8 + 12 + 16 + 20 = 56$ minutes.
It took Wes **56** minutes.

Test 4 — pages 10-12

1. 6
Divide the first number by the third number.

2. 9
Add the two outside numbers together.

3. 9
Subtract the third number from the first number.

4. 11
Add the two outside numbers together, then add 2.

5. D
Luke's cat is half the height of Edward's cat, and Brendan's cat is
shorter than Luke's cat. This means Brendan's cat is shorter than
Edward's cat.

6. D
Freya only owns 'The Zebra Album'. Freya is also the only person who
doesn't own 'I'm Here', which means Sharif owns this album. Sharif
also owns 'Plant Life', which means he owns more albums than Freya
and must not own the fewest albums.

7. HL
Each letter in the pair moves forward 5 letters each time.

8. VA
The first letter in the pair moves forward 1 letter each time.
The second letter in the pair moves back 3 letters each time.

9. FB
Each letter in the pair moves back 4 letters
and then forward 3 letters alternately.

10. HL
The first letter in the pair moves forward 2 letters then
back 4 letters alternately. The second letter in the pair
moves back 3 letters then back 2 letters alternately.

11. RL
The first letter in the pair moves forward 2 letters.
The second letter in the pair moves forward 3 letters.

12. HV
The first letter in the pair moves back 1 letter.
The second letter in the pair moves back 4 letters.

13. LB
The first letter in the pair moves back 2 letters.
The second letter in the pair moves forward 4 letters.

14. XN
KW and PD are mirror pairs, where the two letters are an equal distance from the centre of the alphabet. The answer will be the mirror pairs for C and M, which are X and N.

Test 5 — pages 13-14

1. 3
Subtract 8 each time.

2. 42
There are two sequences which alternate.
In the first sequence, subtract 4 each time.
In the second sequence, subtract 2 each time.

3. 20
The number subtracted decreases by 2 each time:
$-10, -8, -6, -4, -2$.

4. 34
The numbers follow the sequence $+3, +10, +3, +10, +3$.

5. XK
The first letter in the pair moves forward 2 letters.
The second letter in the pair moves forward 5 letters.

6. UA
The first letter in the pair moves back 4 letters.
The second letter in the pair moves back 2 letters.

7. LE
The first letter in the pair moves forward 2 letters.
The second letter in the pair moves back 3 letters.

8. ZR
OX and LC are mirror pairs, where the two letters are an equal distance from the centre of the alphabet. The answer will be the mirror pairs for A and I, which are Z and R.

9. 42
$37 + 5 = 42$

10. 23
$4 \times 7 - 5 = 23$

11. 19
$13 + 14 - 8 = 19$

12. 8
$10 + 21 = 31, 31 = 39 - 8$

13. JOKER
To get from the code to the word, move each letter back 2.

14. COMB
To get from the code to the word, move the letters in the sequence $+2, -5, +2, -5$.

15. SFUP
To get from the word to the code, move the letters in the sequence $+3, +5, +3, +5$.

16. SVERR
To get from the word to the code, move the letters in the sequence $+2, +1, 0, -1, -2$.

Test 6 — pages 15-16

1. 6521
$C = 6, E = 5, N = 2, T = 1$

2. 1521
$T = 1, E = 5, N = 2, T = 1$

3. HINT
$H = 3, I = 4, N = 2, T = 1$

4. B
$12 \div 3 = 4, B = 4$

5. E
$10 \times 3 - 12 = 18, E = 18$

6. E
$12 + 8 - 6 = 14, E = 14$

7. D
$24 \div 3 + 8 = 16, D = 16$

8. D
$40 \div 10 \times 5 + 11 = 31, D = 31$

9. UKQJC
To get from the word to the code, move each letter back 4.

10. AWFUL
To get from the code to the word, move the letters in the sequence $-1, +2, -1, +2, -1$.

11. WQPKH
To get from the word to the code, move the letters in the sequence $+4, +2, +4, +2, +4$.

12. TOLL
To get from the code to the word, move the letters in the sequence $+2, +3, +4, +5$.

13. SX
Each letter in the pair moves forward 3 letters each time.

14. DW
The first letter in the pair moves back 3 letters each time.
The second letter in the pair moves forward 3 letters each time.

15. QJ
Each letter in the pair moves forward 1 letter and then forward 3 letters alternately.

16. RC
The first letter in the pair moves back 3 letters then forward 5 letters alternately. The second letter in the pair moves back 3 letters each time.

Answers

Test 7 — pages 17-18

1.   49
Add 9 each time.

2.   17
There are two sequences which alternate.
In the first sequence, subtract 10 each time.
In the second sequence, subtract 1 each time.

3.   56
The number added decreases by 1 each time:
+5, +4, +3, +2, +1.

4.   73
The numbers follow the sequence −2, −1, 0, +1, +2.

5.   36
The numbers follow the sequence +3, +8, +3, +8, +3.

6.   5431
S = 5, A = 4, I = 3, L = 1

7.   6412
H = 6, A = 4, L = 1, T = 2

8.   LAST
L = 1, A = 4, S = 5, T = 2

9.   DH
The first letter in the pair moves forward 3 letters.
The second letter in the pair moves forward 5 letters.

10.   FK
The first letter in the pair moves back 2 letters.
The second letter in the pair moves back 5 letters.

11.   SK
The first letter in the pair moves forward 2 letters.
The second letter in the pair moves back 5 letters.

12.   WY
NF and MU are mirror pairs, where the two letters are an
equal distance from the centre of the alphabet. The answer
will be the mirror pairs for D and B, which are W and Y.

13.   C
19 − 6 = 13, C = 13

14.   B
27 ÷ 9 + 4 = 7, B = 7

15.   A
9 + 7 − 13 = 3, A = 3

16.   C
24 ÷ 6 + 5 − 3 = 6, C = 6

Puzzles 2 — page 19

Pirate Pop Songs
SEEDS = 27732
BREAD = 41753
SUITE = 26897
Percy is singing about: **BURIED TREASURE**.

A Case for Cluelo
Georgia painted over the picture in the art gallery. She claimed
she went to the rooftop cafe for a drink, but Claude said that he
and Melina went to get food after being told that everything above
Floor 4 was closed, meaning the roof would have also been closed.
Claude's statement is supported by Melina, because she also said
that they left the gallery together to get some food.

Test 8 — pages 20-21

1.   KJ
Each letter in the pair moves forward 5 letters.

2.   RQ
The first letter in the pair moves forward 3 letters.
The second letter in the pair moves forward 4 letters.

3.   NU
The first letter in the pair moves back 1 letter.
The second letter in the pair moves back 3 letters.

4.   AM
The first letter in the pair moves back 4 letters.
The second letter in the pair moves forward 5 letters.

5.   6
Subtract 7 each time.

6.   83
The number subtracted increases by 1 each time:
−1, −2, −3, −4, −5.

7.   28
There are two sequences which alternate. In the first sequence,
add 3 each time. In the second sequence, subtract 4 each time.

8.   25
The numbers follow the sequence +3, +5, +3, +5, +3.

9.   41
29 + 12 = 41

10.   20
88 ÷ 8 + 9 = 20

11.   28
14 + 17 − 3 = 28

12.   3
18 ÷ 3 = 6, 6 = 2 × 3

13.   EULFN
To get from the word to the code, move each letter forward 3.

14.   DARK
To get from the code to the word, move the letters in the sequence
+2, −3, +2, −3.

15.   TNOL
To get from the word to the code, move the letters in the sequence
−3, −1, −3, −1.

16.   QWUI
To get from the word to the code, move the letters in the sequence
+1, +2, +3, +4.

Test 9 — pages 22-24

1.   GY
Each letter in the pair moves back 3 letters each time.

2.   ND
The first letter in the pair moves back 1 letter each time.
The second letter in the pair moves back 4 letters each time.

3.   FW
The first letter in the pair moves back 1 letter each time.
The second letter in the pair moves forward 3 letters each time.

4.   RO
Each letter in the pair moves forward 2 letters
and then forward 3 letters alternately.

5.   JC
The first letter in the pair moves back 2 letters each time.
The second letter in the pair moves in the sequence
+2, +1, 0, −1, −2.

6.   C
36 ÷ 3 = 12, C = 12

7.   E
9 + 12 − 6 = 15, E = 15

8.   A
10 + 9 − 14 = 5, A = 5

9.   D
18 ÷ 9 × 4 + 7 = 15, D = 15

10.   D
Tay reads nine books. Erik reads three more books than Tay, so he
reads 12 books. Devveena reads one book fewer than Tay, so she
reads eight books. Therefore, Erik can't have read fewer books
than Devveena.

11.   E
Faisal is the only person who owns sticker three. Tasha also
owns a sticker that none of the others have. This means there
are at least two stickers that are owned by only one person.

12.   1642
O = 1, A = 6, T = 4, S = 2

13.   1315
O = 1, B = 3, O = 1, E = 5

14.   TABS
T = 4, A = 6, B = 3, S = 2

Test 10 — pages 25-27

1.   7
Subtract the third number from the first number.

2.   13
Add the two outside numbers together.

3.   5
Multiply the first number by 2, then subtract the third number.

4.   14
Multiply the two outside numbers together, then subtract 1.

5.   FA
Each letter in the pair moves back 4 letters each time.

6.   XC
The first letter in the pair moves forward 2 letters each time.
The second letter in the pair moves back 3 letters each time.

7.   OB
Each letter in the pair moves back 3 letters
and then forward 2 letters alternately.

8.   BM
The first letter in the pair moves in the sequence −1, −2, −3, −4, −5.
The second letter in the pair moves forward 2 letters each time.

9.   B
18 − 12 = 6, B = 6

10.   A
8 + 5 − 11 = 2, A = 2

11.   E
8 × 4 − 16 = 16, E = 16

12.   A
15 ÷ 3 + 5 − 7 = 3, A = 3

13.   A
Amica swam 40 laps. Lace swam half the number of laps as Amica,
so she swam 20 laps. Dale swam five laps more than Lace, so Dale
swam 25 laps.

14.   D
Ling wears four items of clothing and Isla wears one fewer item
of clothing than Ling, so Isla wears three items of clothing. She
doesn't wear shorts, and she can't be wearing trunks because Rob
is the only person to wear trunks. Therefore, she must be wearing
the three remaining items of clothing — a swimming costume,
goggles and a hat.

Test 11 — pages 28-29

1. E
$13 + 15 = 28, E = 28$

2. D
$25 \div 5 + 9 = 14, D = 14$

3. C
$2 + 12 - 5 = 9, C = 9$

4. A
$12 + 6 - 13 = 5, A = 5$

5. C
$18 \div 9 \times 2 + 5 = 9, C = 9$

6. 9
$81 \div 9 = 9$

7. 4
$36 \div 6 - 2 = 4$

8. 16
$20 + 11 - 15 = 16$

9. 3
$7 + 17 = 24, 24 = 8 \times 3$

10. 4312
$H = 4, A = 3, L = 1, F = 2$

11. 2556
$F = 2, O = 5, O = 5, T = 6$

12. FLAT
$F = 2, L = 1, A = 3, T = 6$

13. 17
Subtract 4 each time.

14. 29
The numbers follow the sequence +4, +7, +4, +7, +4.

15. 37
The number added decreases by 1 each time:
+5, +4, +3, +2, +1.

16. 32
There are two sequences which alternate. In the first sequence, subtract 6 each time. In the second sequence, add 5 each time.

Puzzles 3 — page 30

Candy Conundrum
Top shelf: 23 — Add the two outer numbers together.

Bottom shelf: 72 — Multiply the two outer numbers together.

Bhavesh's Bikes

Bike Part	10 minutes	20 minutes	30 minutes	40 minutes	50 minutes	60 minutes
Wheel	50	100	150	200	250	**300**
Chain	75	150	225	300	375	**450**
Helmet	31	62	93	124	155	**186**
Saddle	45	85	120	150	175	**195**
Bell	100	202	306	412	520	**630**

Test 12 — pages 31-32

1. 7
Divide the first number by the third number.

2. 19
Add the two outside numbers together.

3. 27
Multiply the two outside numbers together.

4. 2
Subtract the third number from the first number, then subtract 1.

5. SLICK
To get from the code to the word, move each letter forward 2.

6. MAGIC
To get from the code to the word, move the letters in the sequence −2, −5, −2, −5, −2.

7. UDKXD
To get from the word to the code, move the letters in the sequence −1, +3, −1, +3, −1.

8. QUITE
This is a mirror code, where the letters are an equal distance from the centre of the alphabet. Q is a mirror of J, U is a mirror of F, I is a mirror of R, T is a mirror of G and E is a mirror of V.

9. D
$5 + 11 = 16, D = 16$

10. C
$28 \div 7 + 3 = 7, C = 7$

11. C
$20 \div 5 + 4 = 8, C = 8$

12. B
$2 \times 6 + 10 - 16 = 6, B = 6$

13. 3
Subtract 6 each time.

14. 43
The number added increases by 1 each time:
$+1, +2, +3, +4, +5$.

15. 11
There are two sequences which alternate.
In the first sequence, subtract 6 each time.
In the second sequence, subtract 10 each time.

16. 26
The numbers follow the sequence $+8, -5, +8, -5, +8$.

Test 13 — pages 33-35

1. XY
Each letter in the pair moves forward 3 letters each time.

2. OS
The first letter in the pair moves forward 2 letters each time.
The second letter in the pair moves forward 3 letters each time.

3. UC
The first letter in the pair moves back 1 letter each time.
The second letter in the pair moves back 4 letters each time.

4. BN
Each letter in the pair moves back 1 letter
and then back 4 letters alternately.

5. GA
The first letter in the pair moves back 1 letter each time.
The second letter in the pair moves in the sequence
$-5, -4, -3, -2, -1$.

6. 3
$36 \div 12 = 3$

7. 12
$18 \div 2 + 3 = 12$

8. 5
$8 \times 4 = 32, 32 = 37 - 5$

9. 9
$9 \times 2 - 5 = 13, 13 = 4 + 9$

10. 6312
$A = 6, R = 3, M = 1, Y = 2$

11. 3635
$R = 3, A = 6, R = 3, E = 5$

12. READ
$R = 3, E = 5, A = 6, D = 4$

13. B
Li held his breath for 65 seconds and Beth held her breath for
five seconds less, so she held her breath for 60 seconds.
Beth held her breath for twice as long as Jason, so he held his
breath for 30 seconds. Susan held her breath for 25 seconds
and Emma didn't hold her breath for the shortest time, so Susan
must have held her breath for the shortest time.

14. C
Vicky likes lasagne and curry. Steven and Buhle are the
only ones who don't like pizza, which means that Vicky
likes pizza. Vicky doesn't like hamburgers, and Josh is
the only person who likes falafel. Therefore, Vicky only
likes three of the foods that are talked about.

Test 14 — pages 36-37

1. FQ
Each letter in the pair moves forward 4 letters.

2. GZ
The first letter in the pair moves forward 4 letters.
The second letter in the pair moves forward 5 letters.

3. PJ
The first letter in the pair moves back 4 letters.
The second letter in the pair moves back 1 letter.

4. KF
The first letter in the pair moves back 2 letters.
The second letter in the pair moves forward 3 letters.

5. 32
The number is doubled each time.

6. 66
The number added increases by 1 each time:
$+2, +3, +4, +5, +6$.

7. 50
There are two sequences which alternate. In the first sequence,
add 2 each time. In the second sequence, multiply by 2 each time.

8. 24
The numbers follow the sequence $+9, -4, +9, -4, +9$.

9. 25
$37 - 12 = 25$

10. 23
$80 \div 10 + 15 = 23$

11. 2
$28 \div 4 = 7, 7 = 5 + 2$

12. 3
$22 + 3 - 10 = 15, 15 = 5 \times 3$

13. ETCYN
To get from the word to the code, move each letter
forward 2.

14. SLUG
To get from the code to the word, move the letters in the sequence
−3, −4, −3, −4.

15. NRSH
To get from the word to the code, move the letters in the sequence
+1, +3, +1, +3.

16. LOSE
This is a mirror code, where the letters are an equal distance from
the centre of the alphabet. L is a mirror of O, O is a mirror of L,
S is a mirror of H and E is a mirror of V.

Test 15 — pages 38-39

1. B
19 − 13 = 6, B = 6

2. A
30 ÷ 6 − 3 = 2, A = 2

3. B
16 ÷ 8 + 6 = 8, B = 8

4. D
30 ÷ 3 + 7 − 6 = 11, D = 11

5. EILHU
To get from the word to the code, move each letter back 4.

6. COUGH
To get from the code to the word, move the letters in the sequence
+2, −4, +2, −4, +2.

7. LEAN
To get from the code to the word, move the letters in the sequence
−1, −2, −3, −4.

8. SEAM
This is a mirror code, where the letters are an equal distance from
the centre of the alphabet. S is a mirror of H, E is a mirror of V,
A is a mirror of Z and M is a mirror of N.

9. CH
Each letter in the pair moves back 3 letters each time.

10. PZ
The first letter in the pair moves forward 3 letters each time.
The second letter in the pair moves back 1 letter
each time.

11. UP
Each letter in the pair moves back 1 letter and
then forward 5 letters alternately.

12. LR
The first letter in the pair moves back 2 letters each time.
The second letter in the pair moves in the sequence
+5, +4, +3, +2, +1.

13. 15
Add the two outside numbers together.

14. 36
Multiply the two outside numbers together.

15. 9
Subtract the third number from the first number.

16. 7
Multiply the two outside numbers together, then divide by 2.

Puzzles 4 — page 40

A Penny Saved Is A Penny Earned

Monday	Tuesday	Wednesday	Thursday	Friday
£8	£11	£12.50	£12.50	£17.50

You should have circled **NO**.

Crafty Creatures

Test 16 — pages 41-42

1. 3654
I = 3, D = 6, L = 5, E = 4

2. 1456
H = 1, E = 4, L = 5, D = 6

3. LIED
L = 5, I = 3, E = 4, D = 6

4. WX
Each letter in the pair moves forward 4 letters each time.

5. BB
The first letter in the pair moves back 4 letters each time.
The second letter in the pair moves back 3 letters each time.

6. PX
Each letter in the pair moves forward 3 letters
and then back 1 letter alternately.

7. HQ
The first letter in the pair moves in the sequence −5, −4, −3, −2, −1.
The second letter in the pair moves forward 4 letters
then forward 1 letter alternately.

8. 28
43 − 15 = 28

9. 14
20 + 18 − 24 = 14

10. 18
14 + 22 − 18 = 18

11. 4
32 − 7 = 25, 25 = 21 + 4

12. 11
40 ÷ 4 + 2 = 12, 12 = 23 − 11

13. MH
Each letter in the pair moves back 2 letters.

14. BI
The first letter in the pair moves forward 2 letters.
The second letter in the pair moves forward 4 letters.

15. TJ
The first letter in the pair moves forward 4 letters.
The second letter in the pair moves back 1 letter.

16. VJ
FW and UD are mirror pairs, where the two letters are an
equal distance from the centre of the alphabet. The answer
will be the mirror pairs for E and Q, which are V and J.

Test 17 — pages 43-44

1. 81
Multiply the two outside numbers together.

2. 15
Add the two outside numbers together.

3. 6
Divide the first number by 2, then add the third number.

4. 8
Add the two outside numbers together, then multiply by 2.

5. 3465
S = 3, O = 4, R = 6, T = 5

6. 6135
R = 6, U = 1, S = 3, T = 5

7. TOUR
T = 5, O = 4, U = 1, R = 6

8. E
4 × 7 = 28, E = 28

9. B
12 + 11 − 15 = 8, B = 8

10. D
18 ÷ 3 + 11 = 17, D = 17

11. E
5 × 3 + 15 − 8 = 22, E = 22

12. DK
Each letter in the pair moves back 4 letters each time.

13. UO
The first letter in the pair moves forward 3 letters each time.
The second letter in the pair moves back 2 letters each time.

14. EL
The first letter in the pair moves back 4 letters each time.
The second letter in the pair moves forward 2 letters each time.

15. GP
Each letter in the pair moves back 2 letters
and then forward 5 letters alternately.

16. RX
The first letter in the pair moves back 1 letter each time.
The second letter in the pair moves in the sequence
+1, +2, +3, +4, +5.

Test 18 — pages 45-47

1. A
35 ÷ 7 = 5, A = 5

2. E
3 × 5 + 12 = 27, E = 27

3. E
9 × 3 − 4 = 23, E = 23

4. E
20 ÷ 5 × 2 + 12 = 20, E = 20

Answers

5. D

Lucy scored fewer goals than Raeesa and Mia, but more goals than Chris. Chris scored more goals than Andrew. Therefore, Andrew scored the least amount of goals and can't have scored more goals than one other person.

6. E

Betty is the only person to have a black magnet. Roberto, Rachel and Norman all have blue magnets. Therefore, at least two more people own a blue magnet than a black magnet.

7. 27

Add 4 each time.

8. 41

There are two sequences which alternate. In the first sequence, add 3 each time. In the second sequence, add 2 each time.

9. 92

The number added increases by 1 each time:
+2, +3, +4, +5, +6.

10. 14

The numbers follow the sequence −4, +7, −4, +7, −4.

11. HAUNT

To get from the code to the word, move each letter back 3.

12. RKQA

To get from the word to the code, move the letters in the sequence +5, −4, +5, −4.

13. SUHL

To get from the word to the code, move the letters in the sequence +1, 0, −1, −2.

14. CAPE

This is a mirror code, where the letters are an equal distance from the centre of the alphabet. C is a mirror of X, A is a mirror of Z, P is a mirror of K and E is a mirror of V.

Test 19 — pages 48-49

1. FRZXJ

To get from the word to the code, move each letter forward 5.

2. WHISK

To get from the code to the word, move the letters in the sequence +3, +2, +3, +2, +3.

3. COMET

To get from the code to the word, move the letters in the sequence −1, −2, −3, −4, −5.

4. RING

This is a mirror code, where the letters are an equal distance from the centre of the alphabet. R is a mirror of I, I is a mirror of R, N is a mirror of M and G is a mirror of T.

5. 16

30 − 14 = 16

6. 25

3 × 4 + 13 = 25

7. 8

6 + 26 = 32, 32 = 40 − 8

8. 6

25 ÷ 5 + 7 = 12, 12 = 2 × 6

9. SJ

Each letter in the pair moves forward 2 letters.

10. KM

The first letter in the pair moves forward 5 letters. The second letter in the pair moves forward 2 letters.

11. WF

The first letter in the pair moves forward 5 letters. The second letter in the pair moves back 1 letter.

12. QH

YK and BP are mirror pairs, where the two letters are an equal distance from the centre of the alphabet. The answer will be the mirror pairs for J and S, which are Q and H.

13. 62

There are two sequences which alternate. In the first sequence, add 10 each time. In the second sequence, subtract 10 each time.

14. 46

Add 7 each time.

15. 79

The number added increases by 1 each time:
+3, +4, +5, +6, +7.

16. 37

The numbers follow the sequence +8, −1, +8, −1, +8.

Puzzles 5 — page 50

Suzie's Seashells

	Cockles	Nutmegs	Scallops	Conches
Number owned	2	4	8	3

Sneaky Spy

N K H **E** B — Each letter moves back 3 letters each time.

ABD F**G**I KL**N** PQS — Each letter moves forward 5 letters each time.

B EF IJ**K** NOPQ — Each letter moves in the sequence +3, +4, +5. An extra letter is added to the sequence each time.

XD **U**H RL OP LT — The first letter in the pair moves back 3 letters each time. The second letter in the pair moves forward 4 letters each time.

The location of the next mission is the **JUNGLE**.

Test 20 — pages 51-53

1.   E
$8 + 11 = 19, E = 19$

2.   C
$13 + 4 - 6 = 11, C = 11$

3.   D
$3 \times 7 - 2 = 19, D = 19$

4.   D
$20 \div 5 + 6 - 3 = 7, D = 7$

5.   C
Chloe is standing in front of Anele and Tim, and Mark is standing in front of Chloe. Karl is also standing in front of Chloe. As Mark is not at the front of the line, he must be standing behind Karl.

6.   B
Everyone except Stacey and Uzair takes a banana to school, so Peter and Lizzie both take a banana. Peter and Lizzie both take a kiwi, but Peter also takes an orange. As Peter takes three pieces of fruit and Lizzie only takes two, Peter takes one more type of fruit.

7.   1642
$N = 1, O = 6, D = 4, E = 2$

8.   3246
$R = 3, E = 2, D = 4, O = 6$

9.   LORD
$L = 5, O = 6, R = 3, D = 4$

10.   13
Subtract 5 each time.

11.   70
The numbers follow the sequence $-1, 0, +1, +2, +3$.

12.   7
There are two sequences which alternate. In the first sequence, subtract 5 each time. In the second sequence, add 6 each time.

13.   39
The numbers follow the sequence $+4, +10, +4, +10, +4$.

14.   11
There are two sequences which alternate. In the first sequence, subtract 4 each time. In the second sequence, add 10 each time.

Test 21 — pages 54-56

1.   5
Subtract the third number from the first number.

2.   3
Divide the first number by the third number.

3.   5
Divide the first number by 2, then add the third number.

4.   4
Add the two outside numbers together, then divide by 2.

5.   YS
Each letter in the pair moves forward 5 letters.

6.   VG
The first letter in the pair moves forward 2 letters.
The second letter in the pair moves forward 5 letters.

7.   FD
The first letter in the pair moves back 4 letters.
The second letter in the pair moves forward 3 letters.

8.   TK
BO and YL are mirror pairs, where the two letters are an equal distance from the centre of the alphabet. The answer will be the mirror pairs for G and P, which are T and K.

9.   47
$21 + 26 = 47$

10.   7
$8 \times 2 - 9 = 7$

11.   4
$6 + 5 = 11, 11 = 44 \div 4$

12.   7
$22 \div 2 + 3 = 14, 14 = 7 + 7$

13.   C
Nathan walks further than Aaron, who walks further than Marijke. Marijke walks further than Duncan, who walks the same distance as Robyn. Therefore, Nathan walks further than everyone else.

14.   A
Max has saved more money than Eva. Tshepo has saved £5 less than Eva, so Max and Tshepo can't have saved the same amount of money.

Test 22 — pages 57-58

1. VY
Each letter in the pair moves forward 4 letters each time.

2. JT
The first letter in the pair moves back 2 letters each time.
The second letter in the pair moves forward 3 letters each time.

3. AA
The first letter in the pair moves back 3 letters each time.
The second letter in the pair moves back 1 letter each time.

4. BI
Each letter in the pair moves back 2 letters
and then back 3 letters alternately.

5. LC
The first letter in each pair moves back 4 letters then
forward 1 letter alternately. The second letter in the
pair moves in the sequence +1, 0, −1, −2, −3.

6. E
$9 \times 3 = 27, E = 27$

7. D
$8 + 9 − 4 = 13, D = 13$

8. E
$6 \times 2 + 8 = 20, E = 20$

9. B
$12 \div 3 + 10 − 8 = 6, B = 6$

10. 5436
$F = 5, E = 4, A = 3, T = 6$

11. 1642
$S = 1, T = 6, E = 4, M = 2$

12. SAFE
$S = 1, A = 3, F = 5, E = 4$

13. SINGE
To get from the code to the word, move each letter forward 4.

14. CSJJU
To get from the word to the code, move the letters in the sequence
+1, −2, +1, −2, +1.

15. WART
To get from the code to the word, move the letters in the sequence
−3, −2, −1, 0.

16. YZMW
This is a mirror code, where the letters are an equal distance from
the centre of the alphabet. Y is a mirror of B, Z is a mirror of A,
M is a mirror of N and W is a mirror of D.

Test 23 — pages 59-60

1. 45
Multiply the two outside numbers together.

2. 13
Add the two outside numbers together.

3. 7
Divide the first number by the third number, then add 1.

4. 16
Subtract the third number from the first number.

5. TR
Each letter in the pair moves back 3 letters.

6. QH
The first letter in the pair moves forward 5 letters.
The second letter in the pair moves forward 3 letters.

7. OT
The first letter in the pair moves forward 2 letters.
The second letter in the pair moves back 4 letters.

8. WU
QK and JP are mirror pairs, where the two letters are an
equal distance from the centre of the alphabet. The answer
will be the mirror pairs for D and F, which are W and U.

9. 38
$23 + 15 = 38$

10. 11
$16 + 17 − 22 = 11$

11. 17
$7 \times 3 = 21, 21 = 4 + 17$

12. 6
$18 \div 9 + 8 = 10, 10 = 16 − 6$

13. TR
Each letter in the pair moves forward 3 letters each time.

14. BB
The first letter in the pair moves back 2 letters each time.
The second letter in the pair moves back 4 letters each time.

15. QG
The first letter in the pair moves forward 1 letter then
forward 2 letters alternately. The second letter in the pair
moves back 5 letters then back 2 letters alternately.

16. BV
The first letter in each pair moves back 5 letters then
back 2 letters alternately. The second letter in the
pair moves in the sequence +1, +2, +3, +4, +5.

Puzzles 6 — Page 61

Chef Charlotte's Code
There are two sequences which alternate.
In the first sequence, move the letters forward 4 letters.
In the second sequence, move the letters back 2 letters.

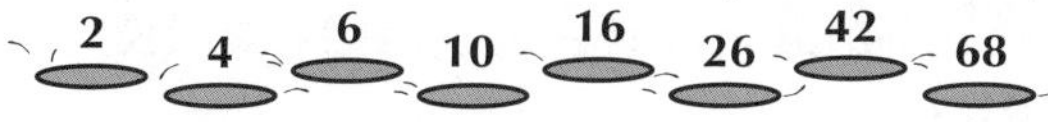

Code	A	B	C	D	E	F	G	H	I	J	K	L	M
Solution	E	Z	G	B	I	D	K	F	M	H	O	J	Q

N	O	P	Q	R	S	T	U	V	W	X	Y	Z
L	S	N	U	P	W	R	Y	T	A	V	C	X

The message says: **Good** work — you're on the team!

Hopping Hero
The numbers increase by adding the two previous numbers together.

2   4   6   10   16   26   42   68

Test 24 — pages 62-63

1. 6312
$S = 6, U = 3, C = 1, H = 2$

2. 1465
$C = 1, A = 4, S = 6, T = 5$

3. SHUT
$S = 6, H = 2, U = 3, T = 5$

4. C
$17 + 4 = 21, C = 21$

5. D
$20 \div 5 + 11 = 15, D = 15$

6. A
$8 + 6 - 11 = 3, A = 3$

7. B
$40 \div 5 - 3 = 5, B = 5$

8. C
$2 \times 6 + 11 - 13 = 10, C = 10$

9. 3
Divide the first number by the third number.

10. 20
Add the two outside numbers together.

11. 1
Subtract the third number from the first number, then divide by 2.

12. 4
Divide the first number by the third number, then subtract 1.

13. RZ
Each letter in the pair moves forward 3 letters.

14. GA
The first letter in the pair moves back 3 letters.
The second letter in the pair moves back 2 letters.

15. DQ
The first letter in the pair moves back 5 letters.
The second letter in the pair moves forward 4 letters.

16. GD
IM and RN are mirror pairs, where the two letters are an equal distance from the centre of the alphabet. The answer will be the mirror pairs for T and W, which are G and D.

Test 25 — pages 64-66

1. IN
The first letter in the pair moves back 1 letter each time.
The second letter in the pair moves forward 5 letters each time.

2. XD
The first letter in the pair moves forward 3 letters each time.
The second letter in the pair moves back 4 letters each time.

3. HL
The first letter in the pair moves forward 4 letters then back 3 letters alternately. The second letter in the pair moves back 5 letters then forward 1 letter alternately.

4. GY
The first letter in each pair moves back 3 letters then forward 2 letters alternately. The second letter in the pair moves in the sequence +5, +4, +3, +2, +1.

5. 4
$16 \div 4 = 4$

6. 6
$110 \div 10 = 11, 11 = 17 - 6$

7. 27
$3 \times 6 + 9 = 27$

8. 3
$4 + 16 - 11 = 9, 9 = 3 \times 3$

9. GRUNT
To get from the code to the word, move each letter back 5.

10. GRPG
To get from the word to the code, move the letters in the sequence +4, +3, +4, +3.

11. STORM
To get from the code to the word, move the letters in the sequence +1, 0, −1, −2, −3.

12. GLNY
This is a mirror code, where the letters are an equal distance from the centre of the alphabet. G is a mirror of T, L is a mirror of O, N is a mirror of M and Y is a mirror of B.

13. B
James balances on one leg for less time than Paula, and Paula balances for less time than Bea, Stuart and David. This means there are four people who kept their balance for longer than James, so he can't have kept his balance for the third longest time.

14. C
Katherine passed the parcel to Caroline and was also the only person to not receive the parcel. This means that she must have been holding the parcel at the start of the round. If Katherine was the first person to hold the parcel, this means that Caroline must have been the second.

Test 26 — pages 67-68

1. 40
Add 7 each time.

2. 66
There are two sequences which alternate. In the first sequence, add 4 each time. In the second sequence, add 6 each time.

3. 50
The number added increases by 2 each time:
+1, +3, +5, +7, +9.

4. 24
The numbers follow the sequence +10, −8, +10, −8, +10.

5. 12
The numbers follow the sequence −5, +8, −5, +8, −5.

6. SF
Each letter in the pair moves back 2 letters.

7. MT
The first letter in the pair moves back 3 letters.
The second letter in the pair moves back 4 letters.

8. MS
The first letter in the pair moves back 2 letters.
The second letter in the pair moves forward 5 letters.

9. DI
XU and CF are mirror pairs, where the two letters are an equal distance from the centre of the alphabet. The answer will be the mirror pairs for W and R, which are D and I.

10. 2135
S = 2, E = 1, N = 3, D = 5

11. 3462
N = 3, I = 4, B = 6, S = 2

12. DINE
D = 5, I = 4, N = 3, E = 1

13. D
$3 \times 8 = 24$, D = 24

14. A
$6 + 11 − 14 = 3$, A = 3

15. A
$6 \times 3 − 15 = 3$, A = 3

16. B
$20 \div 10 + 9 − 3 = 8$, B = 8

Test 27 — pages 69-71

1. YLGHR
To get from the word to the code, move each letter forward 3.

2. RZJHL
To get from the word to the code, move the letters in the sequence +1, +5, +1, +5, +1.

3. HOPE
To get from the code to the word, move the letters in the sequence −1, 0, +1, +2.

4. SZIK
This is a mirror code, where the letters are an equal distance from the centre of the alphabet. S is a mirror of H, Z is a mirror of A, I is a mirror of R and K is a mirror of P.

5. E
Danielle sells fewer frisbees than Rebecca. Zinhle sells four more frisbees than Rebecca, so Zinhle sells more frisbees than Danielle too.

6. D
Millie arrived 5 minutes before Amy and 10 minutes before Busisiwe. Therefore, Busisiwe must have arrived five minutes after Amy.

7. 2
The number is halved each time.

8. 42
The number subtracted decreases by 1 each time:
−5, −4, −3, −2, −1.

9. 59
There are two sequences which alternate. In the first sequence, add 4 each time. In the second sequence, subtract 10 each time.

10. 14
The numbers follow the sequence −5, +4, −5, +4, −5.

11. 28
$4 \times 7 = 28$

12. 15
$10 \times 4 - 25 = 15$

13. 7
$45 - 13 = 32, 32 = 25 + 7$

14. 4
$11 \times 5 - 10 = 45, 45 = 41 + 4$

Puzzles 7 — page 72

Nkosi's Shapes

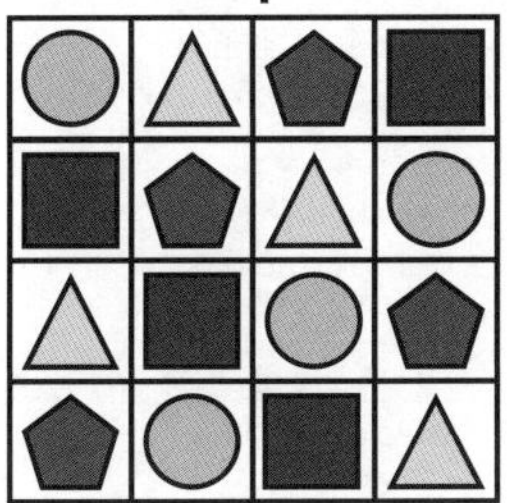

Esmerelda's Treasure

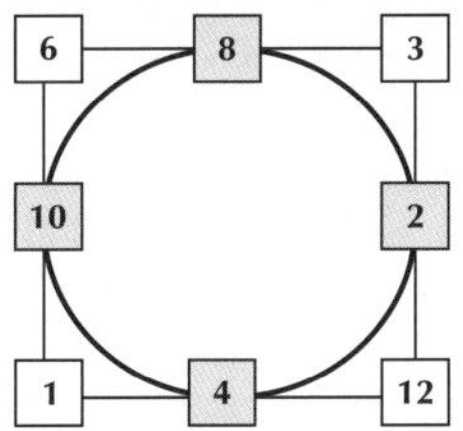

Test 28 — pages 73-74

1. 11
Subtract the third number from the first number.

2. 22
Multiply the two outside numbers together.

3. 13
Multiply the third number by 2, then add the first number.

4. 10
Add the two outside numbers together, then subtract 1.

5. DL
Each letter in the pair moves back 5 letters.

6. WH
The first letter in the pair moves back 5 letters.
The second letter in the pair moves back 4 letters.

7. OE
The first letter in the pair moves forward 5 letters.
The second letter in the pair moves back 3 letters.

8. OT
ZE and AV are mirror pairs, where the two letters are an
equal distance from the centre of the alphabet. The answer
will be the mirror pairs for L and G, which are O and T.

9. D
$14 + 13 = 27, D = 27$

10. D
$21 \div 7 + 13 = 16, D = 16$

11. B
$2 \times 6 + 3 - 12 = 3, B = 3$

12. E
$10 \div 2 \times 3 + 12 = 27, E = 27$

13. RY
The first letter in the pair moves back 5 letters each time.
The second letter in the pair moves forward 2 letters each time.

14. GG
The first letter in the pair moves back 3 letters each time.
The second letter in the pair moves forward 1 letter each time.

15. FC
The first letter in the pair moves back 4 letters then back 1 letter
alternately. The second letter in the pair moves back 2 letters then
forward 3 letters alternately.

16. IM
The first letter in each pair moves in the sequence
−1, −2, −3, −4, −5. The second letter in the pair moves
forward 1 letter then forward 2 letters alternately.

Test 29 — pages 75-76

1. KL
The first letter in the pair moves forward 1 letter each time.
The second letter in the pair moves forward 5 letters each time.

2. VZ
The first letter in the pair moves forward 3 letters each time.
The second letter in the pair moves forward 1 letter each time.

3. KH
The first letter in the pair moves back 4 letters then forward
5 letters alternately. The second letter in the pair moves
forward 1 letters then back 5 letters alternately.

4. RQ
The first letter in the pair moves forward 1 letter each time.
The second letter in the pair moves in the sequence
−1, 0, +1, +2, +3.

97

Answers

5. 1463
K = 1, I = 4, T = 6, E = 3

6. 6542
T = 6, R = 5, I = 4, P = 2

7. PIER
P = 2, I = 4, E = 3, R = 5

8. PT
Each letter in the pair moves back 4 letters.

9. VH
The first letter in the pair moves back 3 letters.
The second letter in the pair moves back 5 letters.

10. JK
The first letter in the pair moves forward 3 letters.
The second letter in the pair moves back 2 letters.

11. MQ
KD and PW are mirror pairs, where the two letters are an
equal distance from the centre of the alphabet. The answer
will be the mirror pairs for N and J, which are M and Q.

12. C
6 × 3 = 18, C = 18

13. B
10 + 11 − 14 = 7, B = 7

14. C
5 + 11 − 7 = 9, C = 9

15. E
3 × 7 + 6 − 11 = 16, E = 16

16. A
4 × 3 + 6 − 15 = 3, A = 3

Test 30 — pages 77-78

1. YLLHW
To get from the word to the code, move the letters in the sequence
+5, +3, +5, +3, +5.

2. SOIL
To get from the code to the word, move the letters in the sequence
−1, −2, −3, −4.

3. OZGVI
This is a mirror code, where the letters are an equal distance from
the centre of the alphabet. O is a mirror of L, Z is a mirror of A, G is
a mirror of T, V is a mirror of E and I is a mirror of R.

4. SALE
To get from the code to the word, move the letters in the sequence
+2, −4, +2, −4.

5. 19
6 × 4 − 5 = 19

6. 4
36 ÷ 6 = 6, 6 = 2 + 4

7. 5
13 + 17 = 30, 30 = 6 × 5

8. 5
33 ÷ 3 + 4 = 15, 15 = 3 × 5

9. XB
The first letter in the pair moves forward 1 letter each time.
The second letter in the pair moves forward 3 letters each time.

10. IC
The first letter in the pair moves back 3 letters each time.
The second letter in the pair moves back 4 letters each time.

11. EF
The first letter in the pair moves back 1 letter then forward
3 letters alternately. The second letter in the pair moves
back 5 letters then forward 3 letters alternately.

12. YM
The first letter in the pair moves back 2 letters each time.
The second letter in the pair moves forward 1 letter
then forward 4 letters alternately.

13. 15
Add the two outside numbers together.

14. 30
Multiply the two outside numbers together.

15. 15
Add the two outside numbers together, then add 1.

16. 3
Divide the first number by the third number, then subtract 1.

Test 31 — pages 79-81

1. 6
8 × 3 = 24, 24 = 30 − 6

2. 10
24 ÷ 4 = 6, 6 = 16 − 10

3. 4
35 ÷ 5 − 3 = 4

4. 7
9 × 3 + 3 = 30, 30 = 37 − 7

5. 96
The number is doubled each time.

6. 30
The number subtracted increases by 1 each time:
−1, −2, −3, −4, −5.

7.   17

There are two sequences which alternate.
In the first sequence, subtract 5 each time.
In the second sequence, subtract 4 each time.

8.   13

The numbers follow the sequence +4, −6, +4, −6, +4.

9.   D

Hazel and Thomas slept for the same length of time.
Cameron slept for less time than Hazel, but longer than
Samiha, and Liam slept for two hours longer than Thomas.
Therefore, Hazel and Thomas both slept for longer than
Cameron and Samiha, but not longer than Liam.

10.   C

Sian finds twice as many coins as Abby. Abby and Jamaal both
find more coins than Hannah. As Hannah ends the hunt with
more coins than Miles, Miles must find the fewest coins.

11.   EXAM

To get from the code to the word, move the letters in the sequence
−2, +2, −2, +2.

12.   BLEND

To get from the code to the word, move the letters in the sequence
−1, −2, −1, −2, −1.

13.   IDEJJ

To get from the word to the code, move the letters in the sequence
−3, −1, +1, +3, +5.

14.   KRXP

This is a mirror code, where the letters are an equal distance from
the centre of the alphabet. K is a mirror of P, R is a mirror of I,
X is a mirror of C and P is a mirror of K.

Puzzles 8 — page 82

Television Time

Travis watches the most television. Teo watches television for
90 minutes because he watches from 19:00 - 20:30. Tamara
watches half the amount of television that Teo does, so she
watches television for 45 minutes. Tasmeen watches 15
more minutes of television than Tamara, so Tasmeen watches
60 minutes of television. Travis watches double the amount of
television that Tasmeen watches, so Travis watches 120 minutes
of television. Therefore, Travis watches the most television.

Captain Codey's Conundrum

% # ? ? + $ * — Walltin
@ = ! & ! # % — Rosesaw
% & ! % $? £ — Weswilk
! $? £ & + + — Silkett

Progress Chart

Use this chart to keep track of your score for each test.

	Score		Score		Score
Test 1		Test 12		Test 23	
Test 2		Test 13		Test 24	
Test 3		Test 14		Test 25	
Test 4		Test 15		Test 26	
Test 5		Test 16		Test 27	
Test 6		Test 17		Test 28	
Test 7		Test 18		Test 29	
Test 8		Test 19		Test 30	
Test 9		Test 20		Test 31	
Test 10		Test 21			
Test 11		Test 22			

Look back at your scores once you've done all the tests.
Work out which kind of mark you scored most often:

Tests out of 14	Tests out of 16	
0-7 marks	0-9 marks	Go back to basics and work on your question technique.
8-11 marks	10-13 marks	You're nearly there — go back over the questions you found tricky.
12-14 marks	14-16 marks	You're a Sequences, Logic and Coding star. Go on to 10-Minute Tests for ages 10-11.

V5LXPE2